modern
MANNERS

modern
MANNERS
Tools to Take You to the Top

· · · · · · · · · · · · ·

DOROTHEA JOHNSON
Founder of The Protocol School of Washington

and

LIV TYLER

POTTER STYLE
New York

Library of Congress Cataloging-in-Publication Data
Johnson, Dorothea.
Modern manners: tools to take you to the top /
Dorothea Johnson and Liv Tyler. — First Edition.
1. Business etiquette.   I. Title.
HF5389.J66   2013
395.5'2—dc23   2012050247

ISBN 978-0-7704-3408-3
eISBN 978-0-7704-3411-3

Printed in China

Book and cover design by Rae Ann Spitzenberger
Book and cover illustrations by Julia Rothman
Author photographs by Carter Smith

10   9   8   7   6   5

First Edition

To Pamela Eyring,
President and Director of the
Protocol School of Washington,
with my admiration

Contents

Foreword

People are often surprised to learn that my grandmother is a world-renowned etiquette expert. I suppose that is because my family is known for being a little more rock-and-roll than Rockefeller. Part of this is true—I was raised by a wonderful and eclectic family, which I am grateful for. But there was something special about my relationship with my grandmother and the things she taught me that made a deep and lasting impression on the woman I am today, both personally and professionally.

When I was a little girl I would visit my grandmother often. One of the fun things we used to do together was go on a "girls'" date. That was always very exciting for me. At the time I was a wild tomboy, with scrapes on my knees, a very short attention span, and a loud voice. She would lay out a skirt and blouse on my bed and teach me the importance of how we care for ourselves and present ourselves in the world. (Oh, and the beauty secrets and home tips! I'll save those for another book entirely.)

On these special outings, my grandmother would take me to museums, the theater, or concerts, but my favorite was when we would go to Bloomingdale's. We would walk around the store looking at furniture, makeup, all the latest fashions (it was the '80s, so it was an awe-inspiring sight), and maybe buy a new dress. Then, as a treat, we would go to the café, 40 Carrots, and sit at the counter to have lunch and a slice of carrot cake for dessert. I remember all of this so well—the way everything looked, the waiters dressed up with big smiles, ready to take our order. Of course, like any seven-year-old, I had my eyes on the prize—that delicious slice of carrot cake. But during those moments before the cake came, my grandmother managed to show me everything about table manners and dining out. She would guide me, laugh with me, and maybe even tell me a little history, such as where the napkin came from and how we are really meant to use it.

These stories and teachings stayed with me. There was something about the way she engaged me that was unique. She was an incredible teacher because I didn't know she was teaching me anything. I was having fun. But somehow I was learning valuable lessons I would never forget. During our time together, I began to see that she had "something special"—a kind of grace and thoughtfulness, a natural elegance mixed with a true passion for learning, a great curiosity, an amazing attention to detail, and tremendous wisdom. I noticed that the way my grandmother treated people had a sort of chain reaction, and in turn, people treated her with the utmost respect and kindness. It was as if her behavior was bringing out the best in them. She would often tell me, "Livvy, always take the high road, because the low road is so crowded." I learned so much from her on those lunch dates.

Recently I found myself attending a large formal event in New York City. Teetering on extremely high heels and wearing a beautiful (but very tight) couture dress that made breathing very hard, I felt anxious as I sat at the elegantly decorated table surrounded by wonderful minds and brilliant personalities. As I looked down at my place setting, my heart fluttered. "Oh my goodness, what on earth am I to do with all these forks, and which bread plate is mine?!" I closed my eyes and thought of my grandmother and remembered our girlie dates. I took a deep breath and thought, I've got this, I can do this, I've been here many times before. In that moment, all the training she had given me just kicked in, kind of like autopilot. I began to relax and enjoy my evening, knowing I could have a conversation with the person next to me without stealing his bread roll.

After that night, I had a sort of "aha" moment, where I envisioned myself standing with a metaphorical toolbox filled with all of the lessons and examples my grandmother had given me throughout my lifetime. Now they were always there for me, in my "toolbox," to use when I needed them.

This book has all the lessons my grandmother taught me and many more. I'm still learning from her even today. As my grandmother always told me, "It's better to know it and not need it than to need it and not know it." I think she's right! This clear and simple guide will help you be the best you can be. Use it and I promise you'll notice a difference in how you feel and how people view and treat you in your personal and professional life.

—*Liv Tyler*

Introduction

Life's a stage, and actors aren't the only performers. Each of us has a part to play, whether as a professional, a family member, or a friend. Regardless of the role, our performance is always enhanced by good manners. Far from empty formalities, manners translate to common courtesy, simply showing small kindnesses to other human beings.

Good manners also show a level of polish that will help you win the confidence of your business colleagues. In today's competitive business arena, your expertise isn't always enough. The ability to get along with others and make others feel comfortable is vital to your success.

This book is for the young professional who is beginning his or her career, no matter what type of employment. It will also benefit those already in the business arena who want to climb the ladder higher and faster. Additionally, *Modern Manners* provides guidelines about how to present yourself socially.

Embrace good manners! They're important and needn't be scary or stuffy—and they certainly won't feel that way once you've mastered them. People often get uptight when they hear the word "etiquette" because it means rules, or they may be fearful of being judged, but the goal here is not perfection. It's to make you feel at ease in any situation—and in turn, you'll be putting others at ease. As the most valuable business tool you can possess, good manners are a solid investment.

Liv and I invite you to join us as ambassadors in the promotion of civility and kindness in our communities and our travels.

— *1* —

MEETINGS & GREETINGS

In nothing do we lay ourselves so open as in our manner of meeting and salutation.

—JOHANN KASPAR LAVATER

Manners enhance the quality of everyday life.
On the job, your training and expertise are important, but be aware that you'll also be judged on how well you handle yourself and work in teams.

The way you interact with people can create a positive impression. Showing consideration for and interest in those you meet, while maintaining a pleasant tone, is the most important goal of meeting and greeting. No matter where you are, there are universal manners that stand you in good stead professionally and socially. That first handshake can be the beginning of a successful working relationship or friendship.

Standing Up

Men and women should stand up to meet and greet newcomers, regardless of the gender of the person they're meeting, at both business and social events, casual or formal. The old etiquette rule that a woman could remain seated when introduced is obsolete; women and men should be on equal footing in the workplace, and failing to stand up signals that you consider yourself more important. This behavior may translate as arrogance, not authority, and it shows disrespect to the other person and to yourself.

When a client/visitor or senior executive enters your work area, stand up and walk from behind your desk when she or he arrives and when she or he departs. This demonstrates that your guest, who is probably not a regular visitor, has your full attention and respect. You may remain seated when coworkers enter your office, and if a senior executive is in and out of your office frequently.

At a large event, only those nearest the newcomers would rise and greet them. If you're wedged into a tight position in a restaurant where it's impossible for you to stand, at least lean forward or rise slightly so you won't appear rude.

liv on standing up

When joined by a friend, even in the most casual setting, like a bar or restaurant, I always try to stand up to say hello and greet him or her with a hug or a handshake. This makes someone feel comfortable and welcomed into the group.

DO apologize if you're seated where getting up is awkward: "It's nice to meet you, Robert. Please excuse me for not standing, but it's a bit crowded here."

DO teach your children to stand up to meet adults and other children. If they make it a habit in childhood, they'll remember it all their lives.

DON'T remain seated if you're able to stand and greet the person.

Exceptions to the Don't

An elderly person may remain seated if she or he chooses to.

Someone who has an injury or a disability may remain seated when it's too difficult to stand.

DID YOU KNOW?

All cultures practice greeting rituals; they vary widely across the world. The Chinese and Japanese press their arms to their sides and bow; Indians press their hands together in a praying position and tilt their heads to one side; New Zealand Maoris rub noses; the French kiss both cheeks. Throughout Western history greetings have adapted to our lifestyles and changing values. In a society where women remained in the background, Greek men developed a rather curious custom. Upon meeting another man, they clasped each other's right lower arms and touched their own testicles with their left hands. This was probably a symbol of honesty. In fact, the word *testify* is derived from *testicle*. In prebiblical times, men swore not on the Bible, but on their manhood (that is, their testicles).

Eye Contact

Eye contact communicates sincerity and self-confidence. It also tells the other person you're listening and alert. The difference between an actively engaged person who is looking at you while listening and a fidgety person who avoids eye contact is astounding—one sends a message of consideration, while the other seems uninterested. As you stand to meet and greet someone, maintain eye contact; if you're not used to doing this, you may feel awkward initially, but the gesture communicates respect.

Direct eye contact normally ranges from 40 to 60 percent of the time. Less than 40 percent, and you appear uninterested, shy, and untrustworthy. More than 60 percent of the time, you appear doubtful and intimidating. Focus on the space above the nose and between the eyes.

liv on eye contact

I think eye contact is the secret weapon of politicians and movie stars. There is something so powerful about a person who makes good eye contact and really listens. It leaves a lasting impression.

For example, when I was a teenager, I met Johnny Depp. Like most girls, I had a big crush on him. What I remember most about him was the way he looked me in the eye and seemed so focused. For a few brief moments, I felt as if I was the only person in the world. I'll never forget that moment and so much of it had to do with simple eye contact. Try this out next time you meet a new client or someone in a social situation and see if it makes a difference. Even if it's just for a minute, take the time to be present and really listen.

DO maintain eye contact while shaking hands and greeting someone.

DO be animated and nod approval occasionally; steer clear of an up-and-down motion like a yo-yo.

DON'T let your eyes glance around the room. That makes you look bored and uninterested in the person you're meeting.

DON'T stare.

DON'T tilt your head to the side—unless, of course, you're flirting. That's a no-no in the business arena.

Body Language

Body language plays an important role in our professional image. Whether we're speaking, listening, eating, or partying, our gestures carry messages that speak louder than words. Imagine someone paying you a compliment while turning away from you, or criticizing you while laughing. The medium—body language—can confuse the message and leave you feeling uneasy and rejected, but the right gestures can make you feel comfortable and included.

Body language includes your posture, which broadcasts your mood and your level of confidence. When sitting, keep your back long and straight. When standing, keep your feet about shoulder width apart and place the right foot slightly forward of the left foot. Distribute your weight evenly between both hips so neither juts outward. Knees should be soft, not stiff. This posture allows the flexibility of a slight movement when necessary.

You can easily boost your presence with calm and natural body language. The less you rely on extraneous gestures, the more confident you will appear.

liv on body language

Body language fascinates me. As an actress, I'm especially attuned to how a small gesture or change of posture can completely change the way people see you. Every time I'm in a business meeting I remember my grandmother telling me to pay attention to my posture and not gesture too much.

DO keep your arms loosely at your sides in a fluid position with your right hand free and ready to shake hands. If you're carrying a drink, keep it in your left hand to avoid a cold, wet handshake.

DO show respect for the invisible personal space of others; keep your body at a minimum of about **18 inches** (1½ feet) between you and the other person.

DO keep a hands-off posture in the business arena; except to shake hands, no casual touching is allowed.

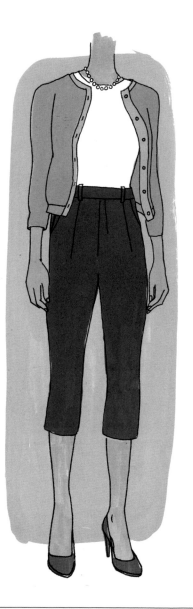

DON'T stand with one hand on your hip. This puts people on the defensive, as it suggests you're skeptical of what they're saying, and invites a negative reaction.

DON'T take a step forward when someone takes a step back. You're invading his personal space.

DON'T put up a "roadblock" by folding your arms across your chest. This posture indicates resistance.

DON'T use the "fig leaf stance," clasping your hands in front with straight arms to form a long V. You will appear shy and insecure.

DON'T put your hands in your pockets. People may wonder what you're hiding.

DON'T fidget. Shifting your weight, rocking back and forth, or touching your face or hair will increase your stress and distract the people around you.

Introduction

I n today's professional and social arenas, anyone who is introduced to another person should be ready to stand, smile, shake hands, and respond with confidence. Despite the fact that making introductions is an everyday occurrence, this simple act can often be nerve-racking. What if I get the person's name wrong? What if I introduce the wrong person first? How do I put two people on the best possible footing? Though introductions may be tricky to navigate, with a little practice your confidence will soar. Then you can focus on each person you meet and not appear uncertain or nervous, and build new connections in the process.

Business Introductions

Business manners differ from social manners in that they require recognizing the pyramid of authority on the job. In business introductions, who gets introduced to whom is determined by pecking order. The person who holds the highest position in a company takes precedence over others who work there, regardless of gender. Business introductions are based on rank, not gender or age.

Should you use first names, or be formal and use titles? The rules of a company's culture will apply. In some corporations, the CEO is known as "Bob Smith," while in others, it's always "Mr. Smith."

In any business situation, introduce the person of lesser authority *to* the person of greater authority. Say the name of the person of importance or authority first, and introduce others *to* him or her. Adding *to you* after the word *introduce* will help you maintain the order of an introduction. Never say, "I'd like you to meet . . ." when introducing someone, as it reverses the correct order of an introduction. *You to* is nonstandard grammar, and the only time to say "you to" is when referring to a certain Irish rock band.

FORMAL

The rules for business introductions are based on pecking order (aka power and hierarchy). Gender plays no role in business etiquette, so it doesn't affect the order of introductions. Persons of lesser authority are introduced *to* persons of greater authority regardless of gender or age. In the entertainment business, the biggest star gets top billing, therefore, the star's name is said first.

INTRODUCTION GUIDE

- Address authority figures first, and introduce others *to* them.

- Say *to you* after the word *introduce,* and maintain the order of the introduction.

- Introduce each person by his or her title (Mr., Ms., etc.) and last name.

- Introduce a junior executive *to* a senior executive.
  Example: "Good morning, Ms. Dole. I'd like to introduce *to you* Mr. Hopkins from our Accounting Department. Ms. Dole is our new Vice President of Public Relations."

- Introduce an executive in your company *to* a customer or client. Clients are considered more important than anyone in your company, even if the client is junior and your colleague is senior.
  Example: "Ms. Hill, I'd like to introduce to you Mr. Dolan, Director of Special Events at our New York office. Ms. Hill is our client from Seattle."

- Introduce a peer in your company *to* a peer in another company.
  Example: "John Smith, I'd like to introduce Helen Marks, my colleague. John is the Office Manager at Hughes Development."

INFORMAL—BUSINESS CASUAL

In many business situations in the United States today, it's a given that everyone is on a friendly first-name basis. However, differences in age, cultural background, or personal preference still play a role, one that is often unclear until the first introduction.

A cautious approach gives you an advantage. Even when the introducer provides both first and last names, use Mr./Ms. and last name, and wait to be invited to use the first name by the other person. Is this old school? Perhaps, but what's the risk—that someone will think you have great old-school manners? The alternative is to risk being known for shabby manners. And old-fashioned and polite is far better than clumsily casual.

* * * * * * * * * * *

It's better to know it and not need it
than to need it and not know it.

—JACK VALENTI

* * * * * * * * * * *

DO add a conversational clue in your introduction by planting a seed to continue the conversation.

Example: "Mary Dole, I'd like to introduce to you John Hopkins from the Accounting Department. John, Mary's our new Vice President of Public Relations. Like you, she's a runner."

DO say the first and last names of each person—clearly.

DO

DO look at each person as you say his or her name—you'll project confidence.

BUSINESS INTRODUCTIONS

DON'T introduce an authority figure to a junior colleague. This reverses the order of an introduction.

DON'T bounce the names back again in reverse order: "Mary Dole, John Hopkins. John Hopkins, Mary Dole."

DON'T

DON'T point to one person and then the other person when you say their names, as they already know who they are—you're announcing, "I'm nervous."

DON'T command people when introducing them: "Bob Hall, shake hands with Tom Becker," or "Bob Hall, meet Tom Becker."

DIGNITARIES, OFFICIALS, DIPLOMATS

According to international diplomatic protocol, women and men are presented/introduced to chiefs of state, royalty, ambassadors, ministers in charge of legations, and dignitaries of the church, regardless of gender or age. This is the same pecking order or precedence established in business protocol; in each situation, the name of the distinguished person is mentioned first, and the name of the woman or man being introduced is mentioned last.

The following guidelines will acquaint you with the protocol of introductions at the top. Are you thinking you have no need for this information? I say, isn't it better to be familiar with it than not? Who knows, you may be called upon to introduce your state senator one day, and you can refer to these guidelines to prepare yourself.

- Introduce a nonofficial person *to* an official person.

- Say one of the following:
  "May I present?" "May I present *to you*?"
  "May I introduce?" "May I introduce *to you*?"

- "Mr. President, may I present/introduce *to you* Mrs. Hall?"
  Response: "Mr. President, it's an honor to meet you."

- "Mr. Ambassador, may I present *to you* Mr. Hopkins from the Capital Agency? His Excellency is the Ambassador of Japan."
  Response: "Mr. Ambassador, it's a pleasure to meet you."

- "Senator Price, may I introduce *to you* Ms. Jones, Vice President of Citizens Bank?"
  Response: "Senator Price (or Senator), it's so nice to meet you."

Note: If a dignitary, an official, or a diplomat has an unusual name, don't fret; you only need to use his or her title, as the examples show.

Social Introductions

FORMAL AND INFORMAL

Social etiquette is based on respect and courtesy, so both formal and informal introductions are made according to age and gender. A man is introduced to a woman in a social situation, such as a wedding, unless the man is obviously much older. In this case, age would rule over gender.

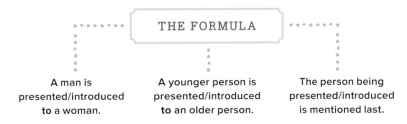

THE FORMULA

A man is presented/introduced **to** a woman.

A younger person is presented/introduced **to** an older person.

The person being presented/introduced is mentioned last.

Keep this easy formula in mind and all you need to do is fill in the names.

Example: "Mrs. Horton, I'd like to introduce *to you* Mr. Hill, our neighbor. Mr. Hill, Mrs. Horton is visiting us from Maine."

Casual/Informal Option: You may choose a first-and-last-name introduction, which is quite acceptable in today's more relaxed lifestyles. It depends on the age of those you are introducing and the degree of formality practiced in your area.

Example: "Mary Horton, I'd like to introduce *to you* John Hill, our neighbor. John, Mary is visiting us from Maine."

Today there is a fine line between informal and casual introductions. See the guidelines on the following page for introducing your spouse and relatives at gatherings.

FAMILY INTRODUCTIONS

Introducing One's Spouse

Avoid referring to your spouse as Mr./Mrs./Ms. in introductions. If everyone knows the last name, all you need to say is, "This is Ted, my husband," or "This is Alisa, my wife."

If a woman is known by a professional name, or has a different last name from that of her husband, introduce her by her own name when she is alone: "I'd like to introduce Megan Richardson." If she is with her husband, say, "I'd like to introduce Megan Richardson and her husband, John Holland."

Introducing Relatives and Others

Clarify their relationship to you:

- "I'd like to introduce Tammy Watkins, my sister."

- "I'd like to introduce Mary Turner, my mother." If one's mother has remarried: "I'd like to introduce Martha Coleman, my mother." "I'd like to introduce my stepfather, Steven Coleman."

- When introducing an unmarried couple, introduce both by their first and last names.

- When introducing peers to each other, say both the first and last names. Do include a conversational clue.

  Example: "Vickie Holden, I'd like to introduce Greg Valdez, my tennis instructor. Greg, Vickie and I met at a seminar last month, and she's very interested in tennis."

Even when everyone is on a first-name basis, introduce each person by both first and last names.

- Group introductions are easily simplified when introducing one or two people to a group of six or more; say the names of the newcomer(s) and ask the others to introduce themselves.

Responding to Introductions

The way you respond to an introduction means the spotlight shifts to you and your performance. Remember, life's a stage . . . and this is your cue to go on!

Say "Hello" or "Good morning/Good afternoon/Good evening" and the person's name. You may also say, "I've been looking forward to meeting you, Mr. Holland." If it's someone in your age group, you may say, "It's nice to meet you, Mary." For an older person, always use a title and last name: "It's nice to meet you, Ms. Morgan." Saying the person's name proves that you were listening.

DO include the person's name with your greeting.

DO repeat the person's name during conversation to retain it in your memory.

DO speak clearly and look directly into the eyes of the person you're meeting.

DON'T say only, "Hello," or "Hi"—include the person's name also.

DON'T say, "How do you do?" This outdated form of greeting is obsolete and has been replaced by "How are you?" But don't use either as a greeting to a stranger. In some cultures, "How do you do?" and "How are you?" are considered impolite and too personal.

DON'T say, "Pleased to meet you," "Pleased to make your acquaintance." These statements are considered outdated and quite impersonal because a name is not spoken.

Introduce Yourself

If no one introduces you, rise to the occasion and introduce yourself. Perhaps no one's available to introduce you, or you may be in a room filled with strangers. You're on your own, and it's time to perform—by introducing yourself. Extend your hand, smile, and say something like "Hello, I'm Marc Stevens." As a guest at any event, it's your duty to circulate and introduce yourself, especially if the hosts are busy. The fact that you and others are present is sufficient to introduce yourself to anyone at an event, regardless of their status. In the United States, you may introduce yourself to elected officials, including the President, the CEO of a corporation, or anyone you meet.

DO take the initiative and introduce yourself to the people you don't know.

DO say your first and last names: "Hello, I'm Heather Wells." This saves the other person from asking, "What's your last name?"

DO be inclusive and greet the people you know, even if you saw them just hours earlier.

DON'T act shy and reclusive by holding back and waiting to be introduced.

DON'T give yourself a title such as Ms./Mr./Dr.

DON'T talk only to people you know—you'll never make new acquaintances, nor will you expand your people skills.

NAME TAGS

The name tag is correctly and logically placed on your right-hand side, near the shoulder. When you shake hands, the eyes follow the line of the arm and focus on the other person's right shoulder area.

REMEMBERING NAMES

It's easy to forget the names of people you've met only once or twice, so don't be too hard on yourself—it happens to almost everyone! When we meet people for the first time, we're so focused on their appearance that we often don't hear their name. This is why we should reintroduce ourselves, which encourages other people to say their name.

DO be alert when the name is spoken and concentrate on the person and the name you want to remember.

DO say the person's name when you're introduced, and use the name often in conversation. This demonstrates a positive interest, and the repetition will help to imprint the name in your memory.

DON'T focus on yourself and your fear of not remembering a name. A little memory blip is all it is, so take a deep breath and move along.

DON'T panic if you've forgotten someone's name. Say something kind, like, "I'm sorry, I'm a little forgetful at the moment; please remind me of your name."

liv on remembering names

Remembering names can often be hard for me. I rarely forget a face, but I definitely struggle with names. A lot of times, people know my name and will say, "Hey, Liv. How are you?" Or I will be greeted with a hug or kiss like we go way back, but I'll have no idea what their name is or how I know them. This can be tricky and a bit confusing. If I'm with a friend, I'll introduce my friend and hope the "mystery friend" will supply his or her name. If this doesn't work, I muster up the courage to say, "I'm sorry, but I can't recall your name. Will you please remind me?" Once I learn the name, I say it three times to myself to help me remember.

FORGETTING NAMES

Just about everyone has forgotten a person's name at one time or another, and then the fear of forgetting further numbs the memory. Take action, and remove the fear. Extend your hand and introduce yourself to someone you recognize, even though you have forgotten his name.

DO remain calm and admit you can't remember a name by saying something such as "It's good to see you again, but I just can't recall your name." If this doesn't work, go to the next level and say, "Please tell me your name."

DON'T say, "You don't remember me, do you?" That negative question can be off-putting and accusatory.

DON'T say, "I've forgotten your name." You imply the person wasn't worth remembering or you weren't paying attention.

dorothea on forgetting a name

Even an etiquette expert can forget a name. While attending a formal event, my husband and I were approached by a couple I had met earlier. I started to introduce my husband with, "Mary and Bob Roland, I'd like to introduce my husband——" I simply couldn't remember my husband's name. Of all the names to forget! I whispered to him, "What's your name?" He glared at me and said, "I'm your husband." I replied, "Yes, I know that, but what's your name?" The couple started laughing, and Mary said, "There have been times when I couldn't even remember my own name, let alone my husband's." She did me a huge favor.

DIFFICULT NAMES

Pronouncing a name correctly, especially if it's an unusual name, shows respect and consideration. If you don't understand the name when it's spoken, simply ask the person to repeat the name and then repeat it back to the person.

DO say, "I'm not sure I know how to pronounce your name properly. Please tell me the correct way to say it."

DO be kind if you have a difficult name and help the person who's trying to pronounce it. Create an association that will help people say it correctly: "It's Hummach, and it rhymes with stomach."

DO be kind when people mispronounce your name. Correct them gently, and try to make light of it: "My name's pronounced many different ways, but the correct way is _____." Your understanding will put them at ease.

DON'T say, "What's that name again?" or "That's sure an unusual name." People with hard-to-pronounce names can be self-conscious about it, so you should always try to understand and correctly pronounce a name.

DON'T make jokes or wisecracks about a person's name—it's rude.

liv on difficult names

Generally, people who have a complicated name know that others struggle to remember it or pronounce it, so don't be afraid to kindly ask how they would pronounce it.

Shaking Hands

Handshaking is a valuable form of nonverbal communication, creating a first impression and sending a parting message. In an earlier generation, the man waited for the woman to extend her hand before offering his own. Today, in the United States, it doesn't matter who extends a hand first.

- Shake hands when meeting someone for the first time, at chance meetings, and for all farewells.

- Shake hands when meeting someone you haven't seen for a while.

- Shake hands when greeting your host and when you say good-bye to your host and other people at a gathering.

- Keep a drink in your left hand so your right hand will be free to shake hands without fumbling and offering a cold, wet hand.

- Be alert if someone extends a left hand rather than a right hand, and shake with your left hand, as his right hand may be injured.

- Be aware that the American handshake is universally accepted, but slightly toned down in certain cultures. (See pages 38–41.)

liv on shaking hands

My grandmother showed me at a very young age how to shake hands. Even when I was six years old, people would comment, "Oh, my, what a firm handshake she has!" She taught me no wet noodle fingers, and the hands should meet web to web. This always excited me because I imagined my hand as a duck's webbed foot. People still sometimes mention how firm my handshake is—even if I no longer think about the ducks.

CORRECT HANDSHAKING

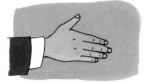

1 Extend your hand with your fingers together and your thumb up with open space between your thumb and index finger. Lean forward slightly, to show attentiveness.

2 Do slide your hand into the other person's hand, so that the palm of your hand rests in the palm of his or hers.

3 The bases of your thumbs should meet web to web.

4 Shake from the elbow with two smooth pumps.

DON'T offer the "fingerella" handshake to anyone, regardless of age or gender. The giver of a fingerella handshake extends the right hand with the thumb down, and fingers curled, which invites the receiver to grab the fingertips. The receiver wants to shake your hand, not kiss it!

DON'T pump the hand up and down like you're drawing water from the well; two or three strokes are sufficient.

DON'T be a "pickpocket" by putting your left hand in your pocket as you shake with your right hand.

• •

DON'T be a "back patter." That may be viewed as patronizing, and leaves people uncomfortable if they'd prefer to have less physical contact.

• •

DON'T use fragrance on your hands; many people are allergic.

• •

DON'T be a "terminator" by crushing the other person's hand. Yes, a handshake should be firm and confident, but this is too much.

Global Handshakes

When shaking hands, as in any interaction, we're not free to act as we please, but we must act with consideration. Shaking hands provides us with a perfect opportunity to express this truth in action. Today, the United States is filled with people from every corner of the globe. U.S.-based corporations and enterprises employ people of various cultures, and often do business in many parts of the world. It's a global economy, and countries we have diplomatic relations with, such as those detailed below, have customs that all business travelers should know. While you might not be getting on a plane tomorrow, this section is included as a reminder that handshaking knowledge will make a difference when meeting and greeting others in the international arena. (When in doubt, follow your host's lead in meet-and-greet gatherings.)

United States
Gender doesn't play a role. A man or woman may offer a hand first.

Globally
The older woman offers her hand first.

European Countries
The woman offers her hand first in business and social settings.

Arab Countries in the Mideast and Northern Africa
Men may accompany their light, lingering handshake with an embrace and kisses on both cheeks. Follow your host's lead. Arabs stand very close when talking. Women are not generally involved in the business arena, and do not socialize with males who are not family members. Handshaking is normal with Arab women who travel often to Western countries; however, it's not their custom at home.

Argentina
Men may hug one another (*abrazo*), and women extend both hands to one another and kiss on the cheek.

Austria, Greece, Portugal, Spain, and Switzerland
Shake hands with everyone upon both greeting and departure. The handshake is firm with good eye contact.

Bangladesh, Pakistan, Taiwan, and Sri Lanka

The Western handshake may be used in these countries, although it may not be as firm as expected. Don't give or receive anything with your left hand, which is considered taboo. A bow may accompany the handshake in Taiwan.

Belgium, Luxembourg, and the Netherlands

Always shake hands with everyone upon greeting and departure. The handshake is light and brief, with eye contact.

Bolivia

Bolivians shake hands with everyone upon both greeting and departure. The handshake is firm with eye contact. Bolivians stand very close when talking. Men may greet relatives and close friends with a hug (*abrazo*). Women may kiss on the cheek.

Brazil

Brazilians shake hands with everyone upon greeting and departure; they maintain eye contact. Greetings are prolonged with a lingering handshake, embraces, and "air" kisses. Brazilians stand very close to one another when talking. Women kiss on the cheek.

Chile

Chilean men shake hands. Women often pat one another on the right forearm or shoulder and may hug or kiss on the cheek. Chileans stand very close when talking.

China

The Chinese greet with a bow, nod, wave, and with a light, lingering handshake. Any of these gestures may be used upon greeting and departure. Wait for the Chinese to offer a hand, and always greet the senior person first. Their eyes may be averted slightly as a sign of respect. The Chinese may greet you with applause; respond with applause.

Colombia

Colombian men shake hands upon both greeting and departure. Women clasp forearms.

Denmark, Finland, Ireland, Norway, and Sweden

Everyone shakes hands upon greeting and departure. The handshake is firm but brief, with eye contact.

Ecuador and Peru

Men shake hands upon greeting and departure, and may embrace. Women who are friends kiss on the cheek.

France

Shake hands with everyone upon both greeting and departure. The handshake is light and brief. A man may offer his hand to a woman, and he may "kiss" the top of her hand. Friends and family may hug and kiss both cheeks.

Germany

Shake hands with everyone upon both greeting and departure. The handshake will be firm but brief. Don't leave one hand in a pocket: it's considered very rude (akin to the "pickpocket" handshake in the United States).

Great Britain

A light handshake is standard in business. One shakes hands upon greeting and departure from a meeting or when visiting a home; however, a handshake is not always correct at social gatherings. Be aware of what others are doing. A man waits for a woman to offer her hand first. The English do not consider themselves Europeans.

India

Physical contact between Indian men and women is avoided in the Hindu culture. The traditional Indian greeting is "*Namaste,*" said with the palms of both hands together at the chest, with a slight bow of the head.

Italy

Shake hands with everyone upon greeting and departure. The handshake is firm with good eye contact, and may be accompanied with a grasp of the arm by the other hand. A man waits for a woman to offer her hand first.

Japan

The Japanese greet with a bow and a light handshake. A bow should be returned with a bow. A slight bow or a nod of the head and eyes cast down is an acceptable greeting from Westerners. Failing to acknowledge a bow is akin to refusing a handshake: the bow expresses respect, appreciation, apology, and congratulations. The Western-educated Japanese will shake hands and make eye contact, as it is more common in the business arena.

Malaysia

Handshaking is not common; however, you may find handshaking in a business meeting with Westerners. Wait for a senior person to initiate the handshake, which will be light.

Maldives, Macau, and Indonesia

The Western handshake may be used in these countries, although it may not be as firm. Avoid giving or receiving anything with your left hand, which is considered taboo.

Morocco

Men shake hands when greeting. The handshake is light, and one might touch the heart after the handshake to express pleasure at seeing the other person or to show personal warmth. Close friends and relatives greet by brushing or kissing cheeks.

Nigeria

There are a large number of ethnic groups so customs vary; however, wait for a senior person to initiate a handshake.

Paraguay

Men and women shake hands upon both greeting and departure, and kiss twice when meeting with family and friends.

Russia

Russians greet one another with a firm handshake, and relatives and close friends are greeted with an embrace and kisses on both cheeks. Don't shake hands over a threshold as it is considered bad luck; always step into the room to shake hands.

Singapore

Singapore has three major ethnic groups: Chinese, Malay, and Indian, and each has its own cultural and religious traditions. A handshake is the most common form of greeting with the young or Western-educated. See the China, Malaysia, and India sections for more specifics.

South Africa

South Africans are talkative when meeting one another, accompanied by handshaking and backslapping.

South Korea

Men greet one another with a slight bow and a handshake. To show respect, support your right forearm with your left hand. Wait for the senior person to offer his hand first. Maintain eye contact with persons of the same level or authority. Women usually nod and rarely shake hands, and they don't shake hands with men.

Thailand

The traditional greeting is the *wai*—the palms of both hands together with the fingers held upward in front of one's face. In business meetings, expect that the Western handshake will be used. Wait for the senior person to initiate a handshake.

Conversation

Conversation is the core of communication, and it takes practice—not just what we talk about, but how we go about talking. The more we do it, the better we become, and the easier it is. Our confidence and comfort levels grow, and we can better establish a rapport and connections with our coworkers, bosses, clients, family, and friends. However, because of a passion for texting, e-mail, Facebook, and other media, many people don't know how to make the most of their face-to-face conversations.

A good communicator opens the door to a response and invites the other person to join in. After the door is opened, the key to a positive conversation is the ability to listen. Yes, we all have two ears, but that doesn't mean we're always using them. Because we're able to process information much faster than most people speak, our attention tends to wander, connecting bits of conversation with memories, ideas, and various other past experiences in reaction to what is being said. This is why it takes discipline to listen to others and *hear* what they're saying.

* * * * * * * * * * *

Appearance is the anthem—
Conversation is the ball game.

—BARRY FARBER

* * * * * * * * * * *

dorothea on listening

At an embassy party in Washington, D.C., I met an ambassador who had just arrived from his country. When he discovered I had worked with his predecessor, he asked me to put together a briefing for him. He explained in detail his specific needs; then he said, "When you are finished, bring it to me."

Two days later I called and made an appointment to see him. I delivered the fifty-page briefing to the embassy and was told by his secretary, "The Ambassador is not available; I will give it to him."

Within an hour after I returned to my office, the phone rang and the Ambassador's secretary said, "The Ambassador will see you in one hour. It's an emergency."

I hastily returned to the embassy and was ushered into the Ambassador's office. "Sit," he said, and remained standing while glaring down at the briefing pages spread on the table. "What is this?" he demanded in a loud voice as he pounded on the table. "It's not in my language. Don't you know I don't read English? Maybe I speak okay, but I don't understand this at all."

I replied, "Mr. Ambassador, I humbly apologize. Your English is very good, and you didn't request it in your language."

"No, I did not, but I asked you to *bring it to me,* not to my secretary, because I wanted you to read it to me so I can understand the words."

Well, four hours and four pots of tea later, I had read and explained every word and meaning. I remained calm, apologized over and over, gave the Ambassador what he wanted, and saved the relationship. That was the day I learned an invaluable lesson: to listen to every word spoken; to listen with my ears and my eyes; and to record every word in my mind. Indeed, his exact words had been, *"Bring it to me."*

As I prepared to leave, the Ambassador said, "I need you to find me a teacher who speaks my language and yours, so my English, spoken and read, can get better . . . and, oh yes, please bring the teacher to me."

I replied, "Yes, Mr. Ambassador, I shall find the right teacher for you, and I shall bring the teacher to you." We shook hands and parted in the most diplomatic way.

Listen Up!

The key to the art of conversation is the ability to listen. When someone else is speaking, you should appear interested, open, and attentive. Show that you're actively listening by giving some type of acknowledgment: nod occasionally, maintain eye contact, smile when appropriate, say "I understand," and so on. As you work harder at listening actively, you'll become more knowledgeable and a better conversationalist. If someone says about you, "He's a good conversationalist," she really means you know how to listen.

• •

DO let the other person do most of the talking. People love to answer questions and give advice.

DO learn to ask the right questions, and people will tell you almost anything you want to know.

DO find some common ground to open the conversation, especially when meeting someone for the first time.

DO use simple, genuine questions that work to draw someone into a conversation and encourage others to speak up and share information.

Example: "How did you get into the public relations field?"

• •

DO follow your initial question with one or two other questions based on what the person has revealed (this is where listening, not just hearing, comes into play). For instance, you may ask, "What was your most exciting project?"

DO be alert as the conversation draws to a close, and include a few comments of praise or appreciation. A successful conversation always has a beginning, a middle, and an end.

DO let the person finish talking before you chime in.

DO remember to close the conversation by shaking the person's hand and saying, "I enjoyed talking with you," or "It was nice meeting you," rather than just drifting away after the conversation.

DO keep up to date on current affairs. Subjects that spark interest—business news, sports, entertainment, movies, music, and travel—are easy to talk about. Armed with one of the above topics, you can simply ask, "What do you think of the latest . . . ?" Political discussions are not foolproof conversation fodder, but if you're in a venue where, if debate is sparked, it can be had calmly and politely, then go ahead.

DO make eye contact because it tells the other person you're interested and listening.

DO listen carefully to what is being said so that you can respond intelligently with your own comments.

DO end a conversation politely, no matter how bored you are. Smile, shake hands, and part graciously.

DON'T monopolize the conversation; give the other person the chance to speak as well.

DON'T finish a person's sentence; you may think you're being helpful and showing that you've been listening, but you'll come across as rude and impatient. After all, conversation is not about "sharing" someone's sentences.

DON'T interrupt when a person is telling a story or trying to explain a situation.

DON'T walk away from the person you've been talking with until you've closed the conversation, no matter how brief.

DON'T brag about your cleverness, good luck, and successes.

DON'T condemn the faults of others, especially in contrast with your own behavior.

Most of the successful people I've known are the ones who do more listening than talking.

—BERNARD M. BARUCH

. . . .

"Diplomacy is nothing but a lot of hot air," said a companion to FRENCH STATESMAN GEORGES CLEMENCEAU *as they rode to a peace conference. "All etiquette is hot air," Clemenceau replied. "But that is what is in our automobile tires; notice how it eases the bumps."*

. . . .

Disagree Using Diplomacy

Conversation often comes to a heated halt over a disagreement. This is because many people don't know how to disagree politely. Some will stubbornly state their opinion; insist that they're right; lash out at others, claiming they are uninformed or being silly; then act surprised that they have killed the conversation. A conversation is not a debate.

Disagreements happen, and sometimes they can even be interesting. Differences of opinion don't mean you can't be friends or that you have nothing in common with the person. In fact, they can mean quite the opposite. Calm down and accept that two friends can gain from bringing different thoughts and feelings to a relationship. They may make each other think and end up learning from each other. Here are some tips to help you take the high road and disagree using diplomacy.

DO

DO disagree carefully because it shows respect not only to others but to yourself.

DO be honest and state your opinion, but not as a fact. Starting your statement with "I feel . . ." or "In my opinion . . ." is the diplomatic way to go. You won't sound like a know-it-all, and no one should get offended.

DO listen carefully and don't interrupt. The other person has the same right to express his or her opinion. If the person makes a point that you think is good, stop and acknowledge it, even if you may disagree with it.

DO explain why you think the other person is wrong by using expressions like "I don't feel that way at all . . ." or "I don't think that's true because . . ." or "Well, I disagree because . . ." This is a very diplomatic and kind way of letting someone know she has a right to her feelings but you disagree.

DO remain calm when a conversation becomes heated or critical, and bring it to a close: "I don't believe this is the right time to pursue this topic. Let's continue the discussion at a more opportune time."

DON'T

DON'T make judgmental remarks like "I can't believe you mean that!" or "That's the dumbest thing I've ever heard" or "That's ridiculous," no matter how eager you are to say them. These remarks will only anger the other person.

DON'T expect to agree after you have disagreed. Instead, a compromise will place both of you on the high road, which keeps you off that crowded low road: "I finally see what you mean, but surely you can see why I . . ." Other times you may simply have to respect each other's opinions and let it go. You might say, "I don't agree, but I still think of you as a friend."

DON'T gang up on the other person and enlist others to your side just to prove that you're right.

DON'T raise your voice.

DON'T respond sarcastically.

DON'T take a difference of opinion personally.

Verbal Padding

Every language has its starts and stops that aren't really necessary for understanding but are used to keep the conversation flowing. Especially common is the word *like*. It originated in Southern California in the 1970s, and became known as Valley Speak. Be aware that repeatedly using the word *like* makes you sound unsure of yourself. Remove this word from your vocabulary and start sounding more confident in your conversation. Many people have verbal tics of which they are unaware: saying "like" or "um" or "you know"; raising the voice at the ends of sentences, which sounds like asking questions; speaking very loudly or quietly or mumbling. To discover yours, record yourself during a phone call. Play the recording later— you'll hear what's preventing you from having a smooth, clear stream of conversation, and you'll benefit from your new awareness.

VERBAL PADDING TO AVOID

Like, you know . . . It was, like, cold . . . It was, like, too early . . . You know what I mean . . . I'm, like, . . . He's, like, . . . She's, like, . . . She, like, fell down . . . Then, I said . . . and she said . . . and I said . . . You see . . . Then I go . . . and then she goes . . . Y'know . . . You guys . . .

"You're Welcome" vs. "No Problem"

The term "No problem" has become a standard response to "Thank you," much to the dismay of the Language Police and others. In many languages, the literal response to "Thank you" translates to "It was nothing." So a reply of "No problem" is not completely inappropriate. But the problem in "No problem" is exactly that—it's considered a negative. "You're welcome," "My pleasure," and "It's my pleasure" naturally have a more positive connotation.

Mingling

The purpose of most events, business or social, is to get people to meet one another and/or to celebrate an occasion. It's a bonus to your host and to you if you rev up your mingling skills and circulate. You weren't invited because the host thought you were thirsty or hungry; you're there to connect and mingle.

Even when you're casually mingling, basic business and social manners don't change. It's your duty as a guest to introduce yourself when no one is available to introduce you. Take the initiative, make eye contact, extend your hand, and introduce yourself to everyone you meet. You'll find it easier to approach groups of three or more, or someone standing alone. (It's hard to approach two people, since they may be engaged in a private conversation.)

When someone indicates she wishes to mingle with others, don't feel you're being "blown off." At times you may also wish to end a conversation with one person and talk to someone else. Always be kind and don't leave her standing alone until you've introduced her to another person.

liv on mingling

It's always awkward when you go to a party and there's "that person" who stands just a little too close. Be mindful of other people's space. And don't forget: your breath is your responsibility; no one likes stinky breath in his or her face. Always keep some gum and mints on hand (but never chew gum in public).

DON'T tell jokes that involve sensitive subjects like race or religion.

DON'T monopolize a person's time. Let him or her mingle as well.

DON'T say, "No problem," when someone says, "Thank you." Never use it as a substitute for saying "You're welcome," "My pleasure," or "It's my pleasure."

DON'T spend the evening in a corner talking with coworkers and friends.

DO make your presence known to key persons in the organization and to your peers at a business event. This is an effective way to let management know that you're a team player and that you support company events.

DON'T say, "We must get together sometime"—unless you mean it.

DON'T make your getaway before introducing someone to another person.

DO end a conversation politely with an all-purpose sign-off like "It's been nice seeing you" or "I've enjoyed talking with you."

DO introduce someone to another person before moving on to mingle with others. When you finish the introduction, smile, lean away a bit, and say, "I must be going. I've really enjoyed talking with you, and look forward to seeing you again."

DO say, "Let's introduce ourselves to some new people," when you're stuck too long in a conversation. Introduce them, then excuse yourself.

DON'T rush to the bar or food when you walk in the door. Slow down and introduce yourself to people in the room.

— 2 —

ON THE JOB

· ·

To raise yourself to a better position,
you've got to do something special
—make an extra effort.

—DALE CARNEGIE

The workplace is the largest — and most commonly experienced—social environment in the world, and no matter where you work, good manners will help you advance, just as poor manners will work against you. It's on this stage where first impressions play an important and lasting role. You're both your own ambassador and the ambassador of the company that employs you. The ability to work with others, demonstrate good manners, and make others feel comfortable is vital to your success. A polite, professional manner will ensure a smoother climb up the ladder of success.

The Cover Letter and Résumé

Many books have been written about how to master the job search; this is a brief collection of tips and pointers for how to make a professional impression. When you apply for a job, you should send a cover letter along with your résumé. It's your opportunity to make a succinct written introduction of yourself, and to show that you're a well-informed and enthusiastic candidate.

Your résumé should be a concise, quick reference of the positions you've held, highlighting your contributions and accomplishments in your past work and educational experience.

The structure of a résumé may differ from industry to industry, but the basic rules of presenting professional information remain the same. Here's a sample that hits all these marks.

- **It should not exceed two pages in length. If possible, keep it one page long.**

- **Keep the tone businesslike and positive.**

- **Two-thirds of the résumé should focus on work experience and achievements.**

- **Educational history is secondary, although important.**

- **Keep personal data to a minimum, though you should be sure to place your relevant contact information at the very top for easy reference.**

- **Unless explicitly asked to do so, do not list salary requirements or current salary.**

- **Never describe yourself in the third person, and don't use "I" to excess.**

- **List your references on a separate sheet. (Before you provide names of people as references, get their permission to receive telephone calls or e-mails, so they're not surprised with inquiries about you.)**

SUSAN GRANT

susangrant12345@gmail.com | 212-555-2134

WORK EXPERIENCE

RAYMORE & HALL ADVERTISING   New York, NY
Assistant Sales Manager   September 2009–present

Promoted from assistant to assistant sales manager, January 2011.
Arrange for meetings with potential clients, and conduct thorough market
research of existing and potential sales opportunities.

DISH & SPOON CULINARY INSTITUTE   New York, NY
Intern, Sales and Editorial   June–August 2009

Wrote sales reviews and editorial reports for a culinary arts and culture
center. Corresponded with clients in the food and food writing world.

EDUCATION

BRYN MAWR COLLEGE   Bryn Mawr, PA
Bachelor of English, minor in Business, magna cum laude   June 2006

Phi Beta Kappa, Beta chapter of Pennsylvania. Distinction in thesis work in
English, on the aesthetics of American consumer culture.

LANGUAGE AND COMPUTER SKILLS

Microsoft Excel/Outlook/PowerPoint/Word, Adobe Acrobat and
Photoshop, HTML coding for blogging. Familiar with Google Analytics,
SEO, hashtags, Klout, and social media platforms (extensive experience
with Twitter/Facebook). Web 2.0, *Words into Type,* and other standard
reference guides and production manuals.

The Job Interview

You may already have met your interviewer on the phone, which is often the first round of screening for an open position. It's cost-effective and typically lasts only ten to thirty minutes, though the rules of an in-person interview also apply over the phone. Next comes the face-to-face interview.

Be aware that one of the most important first meetings you'll have is the job interview. Do your homework and arrive prepared: learn everything you can about the available position and the company where you're applying, because this shows a sincere interest in the organization. Read the company literature on the Web or any reports or brochures that are available to the public. If someone you know within the company offers helpful advice about the day-to-day activities, keep it to yourself. It's poor manners to divulge information given in confidence.

Treat everyone at the company where you're interviewing, from the security guard to the receptionist, with respect. (A quality company respects the opinion of all its staff.) An interviewer will often ask the opinion of the secretary about your suitability, and it's also not unusual for the secretary to express an opinion even when none was requested. Clearly, the impression you make when you walk into the building sets the stage for your interview.

DID YOU KNOW?

Based on research conducted by Harvard University, the Carnegie Foundation, and the Stanford Research Institute, technical skills and knowledge account for 15 percent of the reason you get a job, keep a job, and advance in a job. About 85 percent of your job success is connected to your people skills.

DO

DO your homework and be prepared with details about the company, as well as questions regarding work you may be hired to do.

DO arrive early, familiarize yourself with the building, and locate where you need to go. Use the restroom and compose yourself beforehand.

DO arrive at the receptionist desk five minutes before the appointed time.

DO stand, smile, make eye contact, and extend your hand in greeting when you meet the interviewer, and use the person's name (Mr./Ms. Last Name) when thanking him or her for seeing you. This creates an instant rapport.

DO pause and wait for the interviewer to invite you to sit. If you're not told where to sit, wait for the interviewer to sit first, then sit directly across from him or her. Sit up straight and then lean slightly forward to show that you're interested and alert.

DO watch for signals that the interview is over. Reinforce in one sentence your desire to work for the company. Shake hands, smile, and thank the interviewer for seeing you.

DON'T

DON'T discuss personal matters, yours or the interviewer's. Focus on the job and the role you can play in the company.

DON'T fidget, tap a pencil, drum your fingers, touch your face or hair, or gesture to make a point.

DON'T use filler words such as *like, um,* and *you know.* (See Verbal Padding, page 48).

DON'T speak unkindly of others or another company, even if your motivation is the chance to leave your old job. Focus on the future, not the past.

DON'T pick up anything or try to read anything on the interviewer's desk.

DON'T discuss money or benefits until you're offered the job.

DON'T ask if you may take notes. It implies a poor memory. Write down only a telephone number or follow-up appointment date. Carry a good pen and a small notepad for this purpose.

DON'T use your iPhone to record information. You can more efficiently jot it down using your pen and notepad at the ready.

Thank-You Notes

Always write a thank-you note *immediately* after the interview. The note should include thanks to the interviewer, reiterating your interest in the job and expressing your appreciation for the time given you. (Be sure to send a thank-you note to anyone who helped you obtain and schedule the interview, too.)

A typed note on letterhead has a more businesslike appearance. Today it's also acceptable to e-mail your note; however, be sure that it has the same businesslike appearance and structure. The opposite page has two examples. The first is a little more formal, and the second is more conversational and casual.

liv on thank-you notes

Receiving a handwritten card or thank-you note is always exciting. Even something as simple as an e-mail or text shows your appreciation if you don't have time to write a note.

When I meet with a director to discuss a future project, for example, I follow up with a note letting him or her know how much I enjoyed our meeting and express my passion for the project. This is a very nice way to let someone know you're sincere, and it leaves a memorable impression and sets you apart from others.

EXAMPLE 1

Dear Ms. Garland,   January 10, 2013

Thank you for taking time out of your busy schedule to meet with me yesterday. Our discussion was very informative and stimulating, which prompts me to again express my interest in working with your Public Relations Department. I know I can fulfill the requirements you seek.

I look forward to further discussions. If you have additional questions, my contact information is listed below.

Sincerely,
Mark Haywood

EXAMPLE 2

Dear Ms. Garland,   January 10, 2013

Thank you for taking time from your busy schedule to meet with me yesterday about the publicity assistant position. I was especially fascinated to learn about the ways in which your Public Relations Department has adapted to the age of social media. I'm very interested in contributing further to your department's great work, be it via tweet, Facebook post, or the medium of the moment, and I know I can be an asset to your team.

I look forward to further discussions. If you have additional questions, my contact information is listed below.

Sincerely,
Mark Haywood

Follow-Up Interviews

Your thank-you note has been sent. What happens next?

Be aware that your first interview was probably a "screening interview." Companies want to know if you can relocate, if your language skills are sufficient, and if you fill other requirements.

The next person you'll meet with in a job interview is usually the Human Resources representative or hiring manager, who will be looking for that "it" factor to take you beyond the initial interview. He can ask enough questions, and gather enough information, to let him decide if you should be seen by the boss.

When he says, "So, tell me about yourself," make eye contact, express enthusiasm, and keep it polite. Focus on your areas of knowledge, your strongest skills, and your commitment to quality. Know in advance the key areas to highlight—not just projects you spearheaded or programs you developed but also moments of past collaboration. Many interviewers will also ask you to elaborate on a situation you found difficult or challenging, or to address what you think are your major weaknesses. You can spin one of your strengths into a liability ("Sometimes I can be overly detail oriented") or you can pick a real weakness that you're trying to address ("I'm so eager to get started on projects that I sometimes forget to ask all the necessary questions"). Be honest and sincere, but don't be afraid to promote yourself as a capable, committed employee.

Accepting a Job

If you receive a job offer, call the person who made it and follow up *immediately* with a letter or an e-mail of acceptance. Your letter should acknowledge the explicit offer you're accepting, including any agreed-upon changes. Include your start date. Convey your enthusiasm for the opportunities this new job offers. Your upbeat acceptance will make the person who hired you very happy with the process.

Rejecting a Job

If the offer isn't right, or if you decide to accept another job, reject the position by phone as soon as possible. Be considerate and say how great the offer was and how much you appreciated the effort that went into constructing it, but regretfully you've decided not to accept it. Maintain the positive impression you made during your interview. Follow up your phone call with a letter or an e-mail reiterating your regrets.

When You Are Rejected

Write a note thanking the interviewer for meeting with you and considering you for the job. Be diplomatic and leave a favorable impression. The interviewer might call you at a later date if a position opens up, or she might give your name to someone else.

liv on delivering and receiving bad news

There is no way around it—bad news is bad news! When delivering criticism to an employee, I try to work with the idea of kiss, kick, kiss. To "kiss"—I first say something positive about the person or their work. Then I "kick" them by saying that I've noticed an area that needs improvement. Then I "kiss" again, wrapping it up with a validation and appreciation of their hard work.

Learning to give and receive constructive criticism is a basic communication skill that I think is important. I'm always trying to learn to listen without immediately reacting. Everybody has an opinion! This one likes you and that one doesn't. I try not to take it personally; however, it's often hard when someone's really honest with you and it's not great news. I find there's usually a lesson involved, and ultimately you have to be grateful for that.

Business Attire

Never make light of your attire in the business arena. You may not be a clotheshorse, or place any value on what you wear, but your clothing broadcasts plenty about you, and you can easily sabotage your chances of success by dressing carelessly. It's a given that a professional appearance translates into professional behavior and credibility. People who work with you under the same roof, particularly your superiors, will conclude that the quality of your work matches the quality of your appearance. Especially for junior employees, dressing professionally communicates that you want to be taken seriously—so dress for the job you want.

Know the company's dress code and choose clothes that make you look like you already work there. If you're interviewing at a very conservative company, don't wear a high-fashion designer outfit. Be cautious and avoid extremes. When in doubt, err on the side of conservative: until you become acquainted with how your fellow employees are dressed, stick to muted colors, low/medium heels or flats, and minimal skin exposure. Of course, the industry you've chosen, your job, and where you work all influence your business attire. Financiers, who deal with other people's money, are expected to dress conservatively; fashion designers dress to reflect current and future trends. Colors that look fine in sunny Florida would be a misfire in Manhattan.

Both men and women should plan to dress as suitably and comfortably as possible for their jobs on any given occasion.

DO know the dress code of the company and look like you already work there. Until you're certain of the company's culture, stick to conservative choices.

DO be cautious and avoid extremes.

DO plan your business wardrobe and its suitability for your job, regardless of your gender.

DO select business clothing that is appropriate for your profession, your geographic region, your job title, and the occasion.

DO keep jewelry to a minimum (both men and women).

DO pay attention to upkeep of shoes—leather should be clean and polished.

DON'T make light of your attire in the business arena.

DON'T sabotage your chances of success by dressing carelessly.

DON'T dress for the beach if you work in an office!

DON'T wear inappropriate skirts (such as mini or tight skirts).

DON'T dress seductively by wearing a low-cut or revealing blouse or dress.

DON'T overdo your cologne or perfume.

DON'T let "Casual Friday" overrule your conservative dress when you have a Friday appointment with a client.

DID YOU KNOW?

According to psychologist Albert Mehrabian, these are the components of a first impression:

- Nonverbal communication (body language and appearance)—55%
- Vocal quality—38%
- Words—7%

Business Event Attire

An invitation to a business event will usually specify the appropriate dress for the occasion. If the invitation doesn't, or if you're uncertain about what to wear, call the host. If the event is hosted by your company, call the Human Resources office or the person in charge of planning events.

Here is everything you need to know about terms of dress and definitions.

OFFICE ATTIRE

Office attire makes an easy transition into a business event.

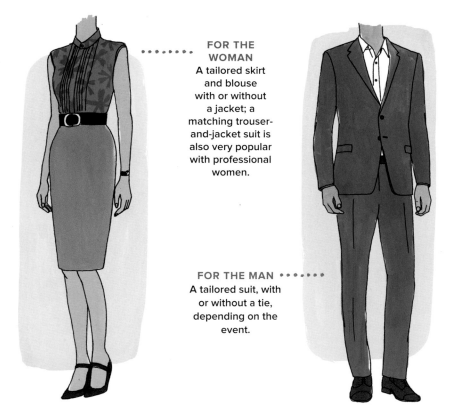

FOR THE WOMAN
A tailored skirt and blouse with or without a jacket; a matching trouser-and-jacket suit is also very popular with professional women.

FOR THE MAN
A tailored suit, with or without a tie, depending on the event.

CASUAL ATTIRE

Casual dress denotes sports attire and is appropriate for barbecues, patio or pool parties, casual suppers, and sporting events (all social events that may be held with office colleagues). If guests are to engage in the sport, appropriate dress, such as a tennis outfit or a swimsuit, may be worn. (Leave the skimpy swimsuit at home if colleagues may be in attendance.) The invitation should indicate whether you're expected to participate in a sport.

FOR THE WOMAN
Slacks or skirts in daytime fabrics; skirts may be short (not mini), midcalf, or long.

FOR THE MAN
Trousers (long or short) and shirt, with or without a tie, with a sweater or a sports jacket (depending on the weather).

INFORMAL ATTIRE

Informal attire means just a cut under "black tie."

FOR THE WOMAN

Before six o'clock in the evening, a woman may wear a dress, a suit, a pants suit, or separates.

After six o'clock, the woman may wear a suit, a pants suit, separates, or a short or long cocktail dress.

FOR THE MAN

Before six o'clock in the evening, a man may wear a sports jacket with a tie or a dark or light business suit with a tie (depending on the season and location).

After six o'clock, the man may wear a dark or light business suit with a tie.

FORMAL ATTIRE

Formal attire means the woman wears a dress, a suit, or dressy slacks and a top, and the man a dark suit before six o'clock in the evening. After six o'clock, formal dress falls into two categories: black tie and white tie.

Black Tie

FOR THE WOMAN
A long or short evening dress or evening separates that may consist of slacks in a silky fabric.

FOR THE MAN
A single- or double-breasted dinner jacket with a black silk bow tie (properly referred to as a dinner jacket, but commonly called a tuxedo, or tux).

White Tie

Denotes full evening dress. The man wears a long black tailcoat and white piqué bow tie, or an equivalent military uniform. The woman wears her dressiest long or short dress, or very dressy evening slacks and top.

Office Manners

Since you spend so much time at work, where you interact with many people, it's crucial to know how to get along with your coworkers and to demonstrate good manners. Just a simple kindness, such as saying hello and good-bye each day, can help create a pleasant work environment. By respectfully cooperating with one another, you build a base of mutual support and loyalty.

While you may form some friendships at work, you should also, in the beginning, be cautious. Simmering under most coworker relationships is a strain of competition. If you become friends, this will also be an element of the friendship, something that must be dealt with from time to time.

Be alert about recognizing the limits of working friendships and avoid becoming too involved in coworkers' professional and personal lives. Use caution and moderation in your verbal exchanges at work—you can be social, but you still need to be professional. Be brief and discreet if it's necessary to discuss personal issues in the workplace. Provide your employer with the services you're paid to deliver—your expertise, time, focus, and work done well—and put your office friendships on the back burner. Good manners, courtesy, and consideration are prime necessities if an office is to function with a minimum of anxiety or stress.

DID YOU KNOW?

A study from the University of North Carolina's Kenan-Flagler Business School states that "incivility in the workplace is the reason 12 percent of people leave a job."

Establishing Rapport

"Rapport feels good, generating the harmonious glow of being simpatico, a sense of friendliness where each person feels the other's warmth, understanding, and genuineness," Daniel Goleman wrote in his book *Social Intelligence*: "These mutual feelings of liking strengthen the bonds between them, no matter how temporary." Rapport—the feeling of mutual friendship and trust—may seem more important for friendships than for business partnerships, but working *with* your coworkers, especially as a new addition to a preexisting team, is crucial to establishing a good reputation for yourself in the workplace. Warmth and mutual respect will take you far in your relationships, both professional and personal.

When you're first introduced to your coworkers, smile, make eye contact, and extend your hand for a handshake. If no one introduces you, take the initiative and introduce yourself. Repeat each person's name when he or she says it. Even if you are introduced to a group of coworkers all at once, shake hands and introduce yourself to each one to create rapport.

Building Rapport

Consider your coworkers your allies—people with whom you see eye to eye. From time to time, you can strike mutual agreements to help one another by actually working together on a project, or in less defined ways, such as by supporting each other's ideas in a meeting or speaking well of each other when the opportunity arises. Alliances with coworkers are fairly subtle, and there may be no discussion at all about such ties. But if you perform a favor for a coworker, you can expect that person to rise to the occasion and repay you when possible, and you should do the same for him or her.

Answering Business Phones

A business phone is answered in a professional and pleasant manner because that voice represents the company and every employee. Always smile when you answer the phone—even though the caller can't see you, the smile is reflected in your voice.

Be prepared to answer the phone with confidence on the second or third ring using a standard procedure, depending on company policy: "Good morning. Global Productions. How may I direct your call?"

DID YOU KNOW?

When you meet someone face-to-face, your vocal quality counts for only 38 percent, and words spoken only 7 percent of the impression you make. But here's an extraordinary comparison: in research completed by Dr. Ray Birdwhistell, an anthropologist at the University of Pennsylvania, those statistics jump to 70 percent for vocal quality and 30 percent for words spoken when the impression is made over the telephone.

When the caller tells you the name of the person she wishes to speak to but doesn't identify herself, say, "May I tell Mr. Jones who's calling?" If you don't recognize the caller, you may politely inquire, "May I tell Mr. Jones the purpose of your call?"

If Mr. Jones is unable to talk to the caller, say, "Would you like me to transfer you to his voice mail, or would you like me to take a message?" If the caller requests that you take a message, take the name, phone number, and a convenient time for Mr. Jones to return the call.

If you need to locate Mr. Jones, say, "Ms. Russell, may I place you on hold while I locate Mr. Jones?" Always wait for an answer before placing the caller on hold. When you return, say, "Thank you for holding, Ms. Russell. I'll transfer you to Mr. Jones."

Make sure you have a voice mail system set up so you're prepared in case you can't answer the phone promptly by the third ring.

DO answer the phone with confidence and a smile, because that smile can be heard.

DO answer the phone by the second ring and no later than the third.

DO ask permission and wait for an answer before placing a caller on hold.

DON'T say, "Who's calling?" (Say, "May I tell Mr. Jones who's calling?")

DON'T let the phone ring more than three times before answering.

Answering Your Business Line

Always identify yourself by both first and last names when answering your business line: "Hello, this is Mark Jones." If company policy instructs you to state your department or title, say, "Hello. Special Events. This is Mark Jones" or "Hello, this is Mark Jones, Special Events Director."

When an assistant answers your phone and tells you the name of the person on the line, greet the caller by name: "Hello, Ms. Russell. This is Mark Jones." When the caller asks if you're Mark Jones before you can say your name, reply, "Yes, this is Mark Jones" or "Yes, this is he." Never say, "Speaking." Your assistant should never transfer a call to you when you're with a client. A client in your office always has priority over a phone call.

The way a telephone call ends leaves a lasting impression. Take the time to end the call on a positive note. Thank the person at the end of the call. Never conclude with unprofessional phrases such as "bye-bye," "later," or "see ya." Say "good-bye," and let the caller end the call by disconnecting first.

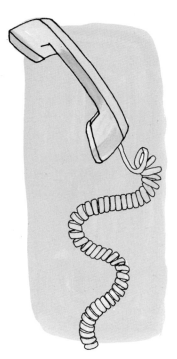

DO identify yourself by both first and last names when answering your phone.

DO follow through on phone requests as soon as possible.

DO take the time to end the call on a positive note.

DO thank the person for calling, say good-bye, and let the caller end the call first.

DON'T say, "Speaking," if the caller asks for you by name.

DON'T transfer a call to someone who is with a client. A client always has priority over a phone call.

DON'T conclude a call with unprofessional phrases such as "bye-bye," "later," or "see ya."

Answering Someone Else's Business Line

Today, many business phones are answered by voice mail; therefore, it's always a pleasant surprise to hear a live voice. If you answer a colleague's phone, do so in the same professional and polite manner you would want someone to use when answering your phone. Answer promptly by saying the name of the person whose phone you're answering and then yours: "Steve Wood's office. This is Mary Hill." If Mr. Wood isn't available, say, "I'm sorry, Mr. Wood isn't available." Patiently ask the caller, "May I have your name, telephone number, and a convenient time for Mr. Wood to return your call?"

Screening calls should be avoided, because the caller will immediately know what's going on. When a person doesn't want to take calls, he or she should be "out of the office" or "in a meeting." It's unprofessional to ask a caller's name, say, "Please hold," then return to say, "I'm sorry, Mr. Wood is on a conference call." Instead, calmly say, "Mr. Wood just stepped away from his desk. May I have him call you back when he returns?"

DO answer someone else's phone in a professional and polite manner.

DO be patient when you take a message and request a name, a telephone number, and a convenient time to return the call.

DON'T screen calls, because the caller will know what's going on. Either you're available or you aren't.

Placing a Call

No one should ever have to ask "Who's calling?" when you place a call. Introduce yourself immediately to the person answering the phone: "This is Mary Russell of the Fleet Company. May I please speak with Mark Jones?" If you have met or previously spoken to the secretary/assistant who answers the phone, a personal greeting is a kind and considerate gesture.

When the person you're calling comes on the line, say, "Hello, Mr. Jones. This is Mary Russell of the Fleet Company. We met last week at the International Council luncheon." Be polite and ask, "Is this a convenient time to talk?" You may have interrupted the other person during a busy moment if you immediately launch into a prolonged question or conversation. Give him the opportunity to call you back at a later time.

If you dial a wrong number, ask the person who answers whether it is the number you intended to call. If he or she says no, apologize and end the call quickly.

DO introduce yourself immediately to the person answering the phone.

DO be polite and ask the recipient of your call if it's a convenient time to speak.

DON'T ask to speak to someone without identifying yourself.

DON'T end the call before apologizing if you dial a wrong number.

Returning Calls

Whether you're an assistant or the CEO, returning calls promptly shows respect to the caller, to yourself, and to the company you represent. Any delay may undermine your present or future relationship with a client or potential client. Project professionalism, diplomacy, and good manners when you return each call.

DO return calls as soon as possible.

DO give a time period that is best to reach you when leaving a message.

DON'T delay returning a call by playing hard to get.

liv on not being pushy

It's always good to give people a chance to get back to you after you contact them. Try not to be impatient and call or e-mail again and again. We often assume that people we're doing business with or the people we love are always connected and reachable, but they may be unable to respond for reasons that have nothing to do with us. Don't take it personally, and trust that they'll get back to you when they're ready or available.

Outgoing Voice Mail Message

Always record an outgoing message in your own voice, clearly identifying yourself and your department. Write down your words and practice until your message sounds natural. Be specific and avoid overdone generic messages such as "I'm unable to answer the phone at this time." Wasn't that obvious when you recorded the message? Keep it short: "This is Marcia Jones, Special Events Director. Please leave your name, phone number, a brief message, and a convenient time for me to return your call. Thank you."

Provide callers one alternative way to reach you (a cell phone number or an e-mail address). You may also specify that the best way to reach you is by text, for instance.

• •

DO record an outgoing message in your own voice, identifying yourself and your department.

DO keep your message short and request the information you'll need to return the call.

• •

DON'T leave cute messages, jokes, or music on your outgoing voice mail.

DON'T fill your outgoing message with alternative phone numbers and e-mail addresses. One option is sufficient.

Leaving Voice Mail Messages

When you make a phone call, be prepared to leave a message. Slow down and speak clearly, starting with your name, the company name, your telephone number, the date, and the time. Be brief. State the purpose of your call and convey exactly what you require in response. Give a convenient time to call you, and repeat your name and phone number so the recipient doesn't need to look up the number or replay the message. Close with "I look forward to hearing from you. Good-bye."

If you misdial and reach a voice mail, wait for the message to finish and politely leave a message apologizing for the mistake. Your thoughtful act eliminates a callback from someone with caller ID.

DO state the purpose of your call in as few words as possible.

DO include a convenient time to call you.

DON'T speak quickly while leaving a detailed message.

dorothea on disconnect and double-check

An executive told me about a faux pas he once committed. He and his team had just finished a conference call with the man who had bought his company. After cordial thanks and good-byes, they joked that the new owner's lack of knowledge about the product would mean certain failure. Suddenly, over the speaker phone, a voice boomed, "Well, that's why I bought your company—to get rid of you." The executive was horrified that he had not done a "disconnect and double-check."

Speakerphones

Speakerphones are a convenience in today's fast-paced business environment; unfortunately, people often misuse them.

Always ask permission of the person you're talking to before you switch to a speakerphone, and explain why you wish to do so. Identify others in the room: "Mary Poole and Hank Murray from Public Relations are here with me, and I'd like for them to hear your comments." If you're in an office, close the door so you don't disturb other people.

DO use your speakerphone discreetly.

DO ask permission of the person you're talking to before switching to a speakerphone.

DO disconnect and double-check after saying good-bye.

DON'T answer a call on a speakerphone.

DON'T take calls on a speakerphone if you work in an open office. It distracts everyone else.

DON'T check voice mail using a speakerphone.

3

ELECTRONIC
COMMUNICATIONS

· ·

I am still learning.

—MICHELANGELO

Today, we can be in touch quickly with colleagues, clients, friends, and family anywhere in the world—we're never out of reach. Unfortunately, with technology it's so easy to fall into the shortcut trap and get sloppy with manners. Recent studies show that many people have become so comfortable with texting and e-mailing that they're avoiding— and forgetting—the principles of face-to-face conversation. Instead of allowing technology to diminish us professionally and socially, we can use this tool as a great convenience without offending anyone around us.

Cell Phones

C ell phones are responsible for the growth and development of international businesses. Your employer can be in contact with you wherever you are, and businesses can remain competitive with this constant connection to employees. Of course, cell phones also offer us amazing access to information and entertainment, as well as the ability to document our lives and stay in touch with one another.

Needless to say, these devices have downsides, too. Our cell phone manners—or lack thereof—affect others. Talking loudly on a cell phone in a restaurant or any public place has become one of the biggest etiquette offenses, as is answering your phone or e-mailing or texting while you're in conversation with another person. Talking about personal or professional problems, finances, and health issues on a cell phone while in the company of others is not only rude but also very dangerous because you never know who is listening, recording, or taking your picture with a phone camera. And remember, e-mails you send last in cyberspace forever.

HOW TO HANDLE A LOUDMOUTH

When you're in a restaurant and a nearby diner is talking loudly on a cell phone, excuse yourself to those at your table, rise, and locate the manager or maître d'. He or she will approach the offender directly because it's the responsibility of management to handle such a situation. Use this same method at a play, a concert, or a movie; go directly to the manager or an usher. This method will help you avoid looking like a busybody and give the offender a chance to correct his or her behavior without the embarrassment of a direct confrontation.

Using Technology
in Public Places

When we go out, it's important to be respectful and considerate of the people around us, whether we're dining at a restaurant or attending an event. When people go out, it's safe to assume that they're more interested in interacting with one another than in staying home and talking on their cell phones. They want to be transported by an exciting live performance, an emotionally resonant event, or a valuable conversation with a friend during dinner. Respect the wishes of those around you; limit your cell phone use in public. Heed the announcement to "silence your cell phones" at the theater, a symphony, a concert, a movie, or when visiting a museum or a library. When you text or tweet during an event, the light from your cell phone is very distracting to others. Cell phone use is also inappropriate at funerals and in places of religious worship.

liv on taking a phone call

When I'm in a meeting or at a dinner, I put my phone on silent. But if I have to take an important phone call, I will excuse myself from the room by saying, "Please excuse me. I need to take this call, but I won't be long." It's never pleasant when a person's phone rings and he starts talking loudly without any thought for the people around him.

If you must have a cell phone conversation in public, there's no need to speak loudly. Keep your conversations brief; unless you're addressing a time-sensitive matter, ask the person if you can return his or her call at a later time. (All conversations regarding personal or professional problems, finances, or health issues should never take place on a cell phone in public.)

DO be respectful and considerate when attending a public event or performance. Turn your cell phone off completely, or at the very least put it on silent.

DO keep your in-public phone conversations short and use a low voice.

DON'T talk loudly or at great length in public places.

DON'T text or tweet during an event. Even if your communication is silent, the glowing screen of your device is disruptive.

DON'T use a cell phone in public to talk about personal or professional problems, finances, or health issues.

liv on finding a balance with technology

Like most people today, I am distracted and at times overwhelmed by technology in all its forms. It's so hard to find a balance between keeping your head up and present in reality and your head down in a world of information, work, and fun. Technology can be very intoxicating and addictive. We all know what it feels like to be a slave to our phones. We look at them first thing in the morning, sometimes before we even get out of bed, and they're the last thing we look at before we fall asleep.

I'm trying to find a balance with it all, especially as a mother, since I'm concerned about what kind of role model I am to my son if he sees me with my face buried in the phone half the time, saying to him, "Hold on, honey." Here are some of the phone/computer rules I'm striving to live by:

- Don't sleep with a phone near my bed—keep it in the next room.

- Set aside specific times to read and respond to text messages and e-mails. I'm more productive when I give myself little chunks of time throughout the day—about 30 minutes—to focus on and get through a bunch of messages, instead of constantly looking at them.

- Turn off my phone during meals at home or out with friends. Take this time to enjoy being with other people and talking instead of each person having a separate conversation with people who aren't present.

- When I'm at work or with my family, I keep my phone on silent or vibrate so I can be focused on what I'm doing or who I'm with.

Cell Phone Savvy

WHILE ATTENDING A MEETING

Turn off your phone's ringer before entering a meeting. Many business environments now require the presence of cell phones and PDAs during meetings, to receive new information germane to the discussion. However, these devices should still have a minimal presence; the focus should be on person-to-person conversation. Set your phone on vibrate if you must take a call during a meeting. Inform other participants before the meeting that you are expecting a call you must take. When your phone vibrates, excuse yourself, leave the room, and handle it quickly.

WHILE SOCIALIZING

When you're out with others, either on a date or with a group of friends, always be considerate and attentive to the people you're with—don't take or make calls on your cell phone. You are there to contribute to the evening by making interesting conversation with your companions, not with callers. While talking face to face with someone, it's impolite to interrupt your conversation to answer your phone or to text or tweet another person.

PHONE STACKING

According to *Digital Journal,* phone stacking is a new game "to get people talking to one another instead of being focused on their phone's content," and it has gone viral. When you're out to dinner or hanging out with friends or family, everyone stacks his or her cell phone on the table. The first person to check the phone pays the bill. A pretty big incentive to keep your cell phone stored away! Here are the rules:

1
The game starts after everyone has ordered.

2
Phones are placed in a stack on the table.

3
The first person to reach for his or her phone to check a text or a call loses.

4
The loser pays for everyone's meal.

5
If no one is tempted, everyone is a winner and pays his or her own portion of the bill.

DO call a person back immediately if your call becomes disconnected.

DO give your phone number to those who need to reach you in an emergency (your company, family, child's school, etc.).

DO

DO make sure, when traveling to other countries, that your devices have sufficient coverage by purchasing an international plan from your carrier.

DO remember that anyone with a cell phone can record what you're saying, take photographs, and/or send messages letting others know where you are.

GENERAL CELL PHONE ETIQUETTE

DON'T talk on a cell phone about personal or professional problems, finances, or health issues in public.

DON'T argue or swear when using your cell phone, especially in the company of others.

DON'T

DON'T borrow or loan a cell phone, unless it's an emergency and you know the person.

Children and Cell Phones

For parents and children, cell phones have become a necessary tool for communication and security. Positive reasons for a child to have a cell phone include convenience of immediate communication between parent and child if after-school activities run late or in case of an emergency at school or child care; to facilitate scheduling a child's time when parents are divorced; and to call for help when a teen driver has an accident. Be aware that local school districts may have rules that prohibit the use of cell phones. Many cities also restrict cell phone use by students in schools.

Parents should teach their children the responsible way to use a cell phone. (This is especially important when it comes to text messages; children and teenagers can send as many as sixty to one hundred texts a day, which could lead to an extra expense on their parents' monthly cell phone bills.) When both kids and parents have cell phones, it's important for families to learn how to put the cell phones away. Establish rules for cell phone use in your home: leave buzzing and beeping devices off during meals, homework hours, and family time. Showing kids how to unplug will teach them how to lead connected but still balanced lives.

DO establish rules and responsibility for cell phones.

DO have your kids turn cell phones off during meals, homework, family time, and special occasions.

DON'T let your children take cell phones to school if they're prohibited.

Texts vs. Phone Calls

Obviously, there are pros and cons to texting (short message system, or SMS) versus calling. A new study from the Pew Internet and American Life Project states that "31 percent of American adults prefer text messages to phone calls. An additional 14 percent said the method they prefer depends on the situation." There are certain situations where a text is preferable to a call simply because it's easier to read a message than to listen to a voice mail. But when choosing a form of communication, it's important to consider the etiquette that goes with it.

Before texting your boss, a coworker, a family member, or a friend, ask that person if you may do so. If it's okay, be considerate: text messages are meant to be short and concise.

THE PROS OF TEXTING

- Texting is often less expensive than making a regular phone call.

- You have an opportunity to review a text before sending it.

- Texting is quieter than answering a ringing phone. People taking phone calls tend to speak loudly, so conversations can be easily overheard and may become disruptive.

- Texting provides a certain amount of privacy.

- You can use text messages to send addresses or brief information to other people, which they can easily reference later or even map using their smartphones.

- Text messages are less hampered by dead zones that may disrupt talking on the phone.

THE CONS

- You may send a text message to the wrong person. Check the recipient's name before sending.

- You can't correct mistakes in a text message that has been sent.

- A text response may be slower, so they're not useful for time-sensitive matters.

- You can't always determine the tone of a text.

Awkward Conversation Savvy

Most of us have experienced that moment when an awkward conversation was needed—and for a brief second wondered if we could simply write it away with a quick e-mail or text. In any awkward situation, such as a breakup with a boyfriend or a girlfriend, or a need to resolve a conflict with a longtime friend, be kind and courteous: have a live conversation, either over the phone or face-to-face. Ask yourself how someone should break up with you: would you want that person to just fade away, or be brave and let you know?

- If the relationship is casual, then a phone call may be appropriate.

- If the relationship has evolved to the point of a real personal commitment, then a face-to-face discussion is required. Awkward phone conversations are difficult because you don't have the face-to-face cues to judge the other person's reaction, and you also deny him or her the opportunity to assess your delivery. Having difficult conversations in person, as painful as they can be, is a sign of mutual respect and consideration, even if you're trying to put distance between yourself and the other person.

- Before you call or meet, plan what you're going to say, and speak clearly and calmly: "I think we should end our relationship. It's not working, and it's not anything you or I did; I just need to make a change."

- Give the person a chance to respond. You don't have to change your mind or concede any points, but listening to someone for the last time indicates that you wish to part on good terms.

Etiquette on the Web

Netiquette is a blend of "Net" and "etiquette," a set of rules for getting along harmoniously in the electronic communication arena. As technology evolves, cyberspace etiquette will also evolve. To maintain civility, follow the same standards of behavior online as in person. It's no secret that we've all made mistakes while e-mailing, usually because we've been careless and in a rush. Mistakes can cost you—a raise, a promotion, your job, even friends. Your e-mail is a company record and an extension of both the organization and the person sending the e-mail. The useful guidelines that follow will serve you well personally and professionally.

- In e-correspondence, maintain the high standards of your company, especially when sending communications from your company's e-mail address.

- Always follow the format of a proper business letter, and check for spelling, punctuation, and grammar before hitting Send.

- Never put something in an e-mail that you wouldn't also say in person to your colleagues. (Companies have priority access over any e-mails sent by their employees, so nothing you send can be considered confidential.)

- Avoid using ALL CAPS when sending an e-mail, texting, or tweeting (it's as if you're shouting).

There are many hidden dangers in negotiating the online arena, but you can inform and protect yourself.

- A good password will be a lengthy combination of letters and numbers, and have no relevance to any easy-to-guess information (such as your birthday, phone number, or address).

- Look into your browser settings so you can understand how to make your Web browsing more secure and to protect yourself from cookies, spambots, ad trackers, and the like.

- When shopping online, be sure to shop secure sites that protect your information when you're checking out.

- Be discreet, as nothing is completely private on the Internet.

- Don't spam (send unsolicited e-mail or electronic junk mail) or follow pop-ups or spam links; this will help you avoid viruses, spyware, and malware.

· ·

DO use spell-check and proofread your message before sending.

DO consider company e-mail public, not confidential.

DO shop secure sites. Know the difference between secure sites and those vulnerable to spyware and malware.

DO use discretion.

· ·

DON'T use ALL CAPS—it's like shouting.

DON'T send confrontational or insulting e-mails, and don't respond to any sent to you.

DON'T say anything online you wouldn't say to someone in person.

DON'T assume that what you post—even if you're using a screen name—can't be traced back to you.

Writing a Business E-mail

Although e-mail may be viewed by some as too informal for business, following a businesslike format is important to maintain your company's image. Always be mindful that e-mails aren't confidential: there's no privacy, and even the signature block is there for anyone to read. In many states, supposedly confidential e-mails are admitted as legal evidence. First impressions in e-mails are just as important as first impressions in person. Your e-mail will be judged just as critically as a business letter.

Use a subject line and be specific about the contents in the e-mail. This will help when you need to look for it on your computer. If you wait to enter the recipient's e-mail address after you've done a check of spelling, punctuation, and grammar, and made sure the correct attachment has been inserted, you won't accidentally send it before the e-mail is completed. Always follow a business-letter format when conducting company business.

TIPS FOR SENDING BUSINESS E-MAILS

● Use a short and relevant subject line to clarify the e-mail's content. This also lets the reader locate your e-mail in the future.

● Keep e-mails short and to the point. For an e-mail with a longer report, use an attachment.

● Check your e-mail's spelling, grammar, and punctuation.

● Always verify the recipient's e-mail address before sending. Sending an e-mail to the wrong person is a common mistake. Double-check and save yourself from embarrassment before hitting Send.

● Include a greeting and signature line at the end of your message: your full name, title, company name, street address, phone, fax, e-mail address, website, and, if your company requires it, a disclaimer.

Since you can't know when the person you're sending an e-mail to will read it, you shouldn't expect an immediate response. Forwarding spam and chain letters and sending useless e-mails is considered not only rude but also a waste of your company's time. Even though we know that there is no privacy on the Internet, people do send "confidential" e-mails. Never forward a confidential e-mail that has been sent to you.

People who send BCCs (blind carbon copies) are hoping to keep the recipient list secret. This can lead to mistakes being made by someone else forwarding your e-mail to a recipient you didn't want to receive it. You can also make a mistake when responding to an e-mail that has a number of CCs (carbon copies): you want to respond only to the sender, but you hit the Reply All button, and everyone receives the reply e-mail. Again, be careful and take the time to be sure you're sending your e-mail to the correct recipient. If someone receives an e-mail by mistake, the only thing you can do is apologize and handle any negative fallout.

DO use a subject line and be specific about the contents of the e-mail.

DO wait to enter the recipient's e-mail address until after you've proofread your e-mail.

DO include a greeting and sign your name for business e-mails.

DO apologize if an e-mail is sent by mistake.

DON'T expect an instant response.

DON'T forward spam, chain letters, and useless e-mail.

DON'T overuse BCC (blind carbon copy), hoping to keep the recipient list secret.

DON'T hit the Reply All button if you want only the sender to receive your reply.

DON'T forward e-mails that have been sent in confidence.

International Business E-mail

Multinational businesses have made it important to be aware of Netiquette differences in other countries.

TIPS FOR SENDING INTERNATIONAL BUSINESS E-MAILS

● When e-mailing internationally, always address the recipient formally and use a title (Mr./Ms.) until invited to use a first name.

● Keep a professional tone and intent to every word in your e-mail. Abbreviations, emoticons, idioms, jokes, slang words, using all lowercase, and even casual language may be misunderstood.

● Use metric measurements, followed by equivalents used in the United States: 3 meters (10 feet). Don't make your e-mail recipient do the work of converting the numbers.

● Use forms for dates, time, and money common in your recipient's country: 15.01.13 instead of January 15, 2013; 1300 hours instead of 1:00 p.m.; £ instead of US$.

● If you schedule a meeting via e-mail, make sure you use both your time zone and your recipient's (e.g., if you wish to call at 9:00 a.m. your time, let your recipient know it will be noon her time).

● Be patient regarding the time zone differences and don't expect an immediate response, as communication with a business associate in another country may take an extra day before you receive a reply.

● Ask permission before sending a large attachment.

● Do a careful final read of your draft and make corrections before sending.

● Be aware of cultural differences in the country where you are conducting business.

SAMPLE BUSINESS E-MAIL

To: Ms. Mary Brown
Cc: Arnold Bishop, Megan Smith
From: Janet Johnson
Date: March 16, 2013
Subject: New Logos

Dear Ms. Brown:

I look forward to meeting with you and Arnold Bishop, our Design Manager, at our company headquarters on Friday, May 3, 2013, at 9:00 a.m.

We are excited about the new logos that you have created, and the design team is looking forward to adding them to our products.

If you have any questions before the meeting, please don't hesitate to contact me.

Sincerely,
Janet Johnson

JANET JOHNSON
President
XYZ Corporation
2590 West 34th Street
New York, NY USA 10011
Phone: 1.212.555.2222
Fax: 1.212.555.2223
E-mail: janetjohnson@XYZcorp.net
www.XYZCorp.net

Receiving and Responding to E-mails

Read all of your e-mails before responding to a single one. Read the most recent ones first because you may find earlier messages have been updated or amended. If you have e-mailed someone a request for specific information, be considerate and e-mail a thank-you to acknowledge its receipt.

Check your e-mail messages with the same frequency that you check your voice mail—at least three to four times each day (morning/noon/afternoon/end of day). Respond within the same time frame as for a phone call: ASAP (as soon as possible) if urgent, or within twenty-four hours. Send a quick and brief e-mail if you need longer to reply. If you're replying to an e-mail, include the original e-mail with your reply. This saves you and the receiver the time required to search out or recall what was originally said.

Use the "Out of Office" message if you're out of your office for an extended time. Provide information about the time and date of your return, another way to contact you (or someone handling things for you in your absence) if urgent, and any other necessary details. Keep your messages short.

ON COMPANY TIME

Be mindful that companies can and do monitor employee e-mail. Employers have the legal right to read all employee e-mail on the company's computer systems. Abuse can be grounds for termination. Separate your work life from your personal life by creating e-mail accounts for work, your friends, shopping, and online gaming. If you send a personal e-mail from the company's computer, it may be viewed as coming from the company.

DO

DO protect your password.

DO follow a businesslike format to maintain your company's image. Remember that once an e-mail has been sent, it's out there for anyone to read.

DO use a subject line; keep e-mails short and to the point.

DO check spelling, punctuation, and grammar; also, verify the recipient's address.

DO check e-mails at least four times a day, and respond within twenty-four hours.

DO be discreet and avoid jokes or off-color remarks that may reflect negatively on your company.

DO take the high road when you're tempted to send a heated e-mail—wait until you cool down, then project civility and call the person you wish to address.

DO speak to your colleagues in person instead of sending multiple e-mails.

DON'T

DON'T forward an e-mail unless you tell the original author first. Note that your own e-mail may be forwarded without your knowledge.

DON'T use company computers for your personal business.

DON'T argue or send e-mails when you're angry; an e-mail argument only fuels the fire.

DON'T spam.

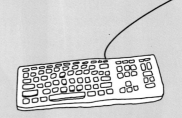

Social Media

In the past, most of us received local and world news through the mainstream media (newspaper/radio/television journalism). Today, newer media such as blogs, Facebook, YouTube, Skype, Twitter, and Tumblr, to name a few, have provided a way for family and friends to stay in touch, as well as a boost for businesses through a new tool—social media marketing. News, whether local or international, becomes accessible almost the moment it happens. When online information goes viral, it can be easily misunderstood or miscommunicated. Be deliberate with your manners when using social media, even in the name of online networking, so that no matter what platform you're on, people will want to engage with you and listen to your ideas.

Always be cautious: there's *no privacy* once you've sent an e-mail, posted a blog, put a video on YouTube, or tweeted someone. The venue you select becomes your electronic entrance to a worldwide community, and being a part of any community brings with it expectations and responsibilities. You're putting not only your face out there for all to access but also your reputation, your credibility, and your integrity. Current or future employers, colleagues, family, friends, or significant others will see you and make judgments about you.

INFO SHARING

Since social networking sites are used and visited by millions of people daily, it's important to project the same manners you would use if these relationships were being conducted in person. A few rules for what information should be shared are essential to making the most of your online identity.

- First and foremost, set up separate sites for your personal and professional lives; keep a polite tone on any professional or social network.

- After you've set up your professional social network site, be it a LinkedIn profile or your own website, be sure to keep it updated with information that will be important for a potential employer. Post content that features your personal and professional interests; for example, even if you use Facebook primarily for social interactions, chats, and quick posts on the walls of friends and family, adding a post here and there when you see an interesting article pertaining to your profession shows a personal investment and engagement in your work.

- Posting all the time, however, can be overwhelming—keep your posts to a minimum and don't overload your friends with too many bulletins.

- While you should use social networking to share your new ventures and accomplishments, try not to duplicate your information from network to network. Designate different networks for different functions.

- No matter what network you're on, never disparage your job or your coworkers online. Both your current and future employers have the ability to pull up online information on you, and even a quick casual comment on Facebook or Twitter, such as "I hate my job" during a stressful day, can come back to haunt you.

DO post comments that showcase your personal interests and your professional expertise.

DO keep a polite tone on any professional or social network.

DO

DO be careful what you post. Keep your profile up-to-date.

DO keep any and all information you've learned about a coworker to yourself.

INFO SHARING

DON'T spam people.

DON'T post more than one bulletin a day.

DON'T

DON'T be mean-spirited by venting and typing things you wouldn't say face to face.

DON'T gossip.

ONLINE PERSONA

When joining a social networking site, choose a profile picture that looks professional. It doesn't have to be a studio head shot, but it should be nonoffensive and convey a true image of you to connect to your audience, especially if you join a site such as LinkedIn, which caters to a more professional business group of friends. (You can use a candid photograph to accompany your profile, but never one in which the setting or behavior is overly casual—on the beach, at a drunken party, etc. Save those frivolous shots for another site, such as your friends-only Flickr page.) Decide whom to "friend," and be selective as you build a solid network. Be mindful that the bigger your friend network, the more applications, events, chat sessions, and cause invitations you'll receive . . . and the more people you have to think about as you screen your posted content. Sharing too much information, such as revealing where a friend is located when he or she wants to have some privacy, is invasive, leading to some uneasy moments and closing off some of your Facebook friendships.

DO present a true reflection of yourself. Fill out a personal/professional profile, and add information about yourself, your interests, your career, and so on.

DO choose a professional profile picture.

DO reserve friending for those you're sincerely interested in and care about.

DON'T be offended if people don't reply to a "friend" request. They may prefer a limited group of friends, or they may want to keep their work and social lives separate.

DON'T use friending as a way of keeping score of your popularity.

YOUTUBE

YouTube is all about you—videos that you either star in or just upload, share, and view. Be aware that your videos must be "grabbers" to attract viewers because there's heavy competition on YouTube. You can use YouTube content as a promotional tool and also to educate consumers about your products and services. Listen to feedback from your viewers and value a customer who takes the time to deliver both positive and negative feedback that you can use to improve your pitch. When viewing a video, leave positive comments about videos you like because the more comments posted for a video, the higher it gets ranked. As the video provider, log in at least twice a week and respond to messages promptly to project a positive image to the viewers.

DO listen to feedback and learn from your viewers.

DO be aware that all feedback won't be positive, because there are envious and unkind people who thrive on negativity.

DO leave positive comments for videos you like.

DO log in at least twice a week and respond to messages promptly to project a positive image.

DON'T post unkind comments about videos, because if you can't say anything nice, you shouldn't say anything, period.

DON'T search for or watch porn; it's against YouTube rules, and doing so can get your account blocked or prompt a visit from the police investigating child pornography.

DON'T upload copyrighted material; it's illegal.

TWITTER

Twitter is a social networking and microblogging service that enables its users to send and read other users' messages of 140 characters or less, called tweets. Use a direct message on Twitter to make one-on-one plans, because your followers don't need to know your individual plans, or take your plans off-line entirely. Follow only people you can trust, whom you find interesting, or whom you learn from. For a boost in your career path, do some research and find out who the leading Twitter members are in your field and follow their content (and their example).

There are, of course, times to disconnect from your social engagement. While attending an event, you don't need to tweet a running commentary about what's happening (unless you've been hired to do so). Bragging about yourself, or engaging in excessive plugging of your work, is the same as spamming in the Twitter arena.

DO be kind and use a direct message to make one-on-one plans via Twitter.

DO use restraint and follow only people you can trust, whom you find interesting, or whom you learn from.

DON'T provide a running commentary of an event you're attending.

DON'T engage in excessive plugging of yourself or your work.

DON'T use foul or other offensive language.

— 4 —

OUT & ABOUT

· ·

Every exit is an entry
somewhere else.

—TOM STOPPARD

You've established yourself at your workplace. Now it's time to be sure you're practicing modern manners when you're out and about—sharing the elevator with colleagues at a conference or traveling via a flight to another city are both examples of when the necessity of business travel and the questions of etiquette collide. Doors, subways, taxis, etc., all allow us to show that good manners aren't dead—as we climb the corporate ladder, or just put our best foot forward socially.

Entrances and Exits

Even with today's relaxed etiquette rules, there's still confusion about who goes through a door first. In the business arena courtesy is gender-neutral, and you should do what is considerate of your guests, clients, and those around you, regardless of gender or position.

Doors

PUSH DOORS

- When you reach a push door first, pass through and hold it open to ensure it doesn't hit the person following you. Hold the door open for someone carrying packages, older people, those with disabilities, and slow walkers.

- A host escorting a visitor in a building unfamiliar to him or her should lead the way by going through a door first. As you approach a door, alert the visitor that you'll precede him or her. Push the door, pass through, and then hold it open.

---

liv on holding doors

My grandmother raised me to be a bit of a "gentleman." When I'm with my family or friends, I like to take care of them by doing things like holding doors for them, helping to carry their bags, or letting them go first. I don't mean to be judgmental, but when someone doesn't hold the door open for another person, I can't help but notice it.

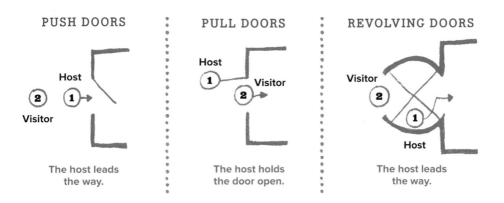

PUSH DOORS	PULL DOORS	REVOLVING DOORS
The host leads the way.	The host holds the door open.	The host leads the way.

PULL DOORS

- When a door pulls toward you, it's courteous to hold the door for others, especially if they are senior executives. Do the same for someone carrying packages, older people, those with disabilities, and slow walkers.

- A host should always pull the door open for visitors and motion them to walk ahead.

REVOLVING AND AUTOMATIC DOORS

- When you're the host, approach the door and say, "I'll go first and meet you in the lobby" or "I'll meet you on the sidewalk," if you're exiting a building. Enter the revolving door to position it and wait for the other person to enter the next compartment, then start moving the door. If you slow down or stop, it throws everyone's momentum off. Once you exit, wait for your visitor to join you and then continue walking. If more than one person is following you, wait until everyone has left the revolving door.

- Always yield to older people, those with disabilities, slow walkers, and those carrying packages.

The Ins and Outs of Elevators

- The person nearest the door of the elevator enters first. Before you get on the elevator, stand back from the door, so those who want to exit may do so with ease. Passengers who are already in an elevator should allow those entering unblocked access.

- Be considerate and hold the "open door" button until others have entered.

- When you enter, move as far back as you can to allow room for others. However, if you're one of the first to enter and will be among the first to exit, step to the side, near the door, rather than to the back, to make your exit easier. That way, you won't have to push through others to exit.

- It's thoughtful of the person nearest the floor-control panel to ask, "Which floor?" and then push the appropriate button.

- The elevator is a public space, so be mindful of your voice level and speak just above a whisper. Only the person you're speaking to should hear your conversation.

- When the elevator door opens, the person closest to the door should exit first. Be alert and courteous when you're in the front of a crowded elevator by stepping out and to the side when the door opens so that people in the back can exit.

ELEVATORS

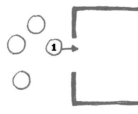

The person nearest the
door enters first.

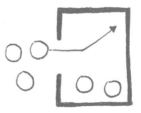

Move as far back as you can
to allow room for others.

Escalators and Stairs

Using escalators and stairs requires alertness and courtesy while you move up or down. Approach the escalator, step on, and move to the right side of the moving stairway so others in a hurry may pass you on the left. When you're the host, you lead the way whether you're going up or down. This lets you lead the visitor, who may be unfamiliar with the area. Before you step on the escalator, say, "Please follow me. I'll lead the way."

When you're with two or more persons, you should stand behind one another and to the right side of the moving stairway so anyone in a hurry can pass you on the left. When you're not sure where you're going as you exit an escalator or stairs, take several steps forward and move to the right, out of the flow of traffic.

ESCALATORS AND STAIRS

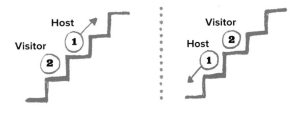

The host leads the way going up or down.

DO be alert and courteous on an escalator.

DO let your visitor know to follow you.

DO move to the right side after stepping onto the escalator.

DO step forward when exiting the escalator or stairs and move to the right to get your bearing.

Traveling: Manners in Motion

When you travel on a business trip, no matter what position you hold, you're an ambassador of the company. Anything you do will reflect on the company. Conduct yourself with dignity and use good manners throughout your travels. Keep in mind that when you travel on business, the operative word is *business*. Always smile and thank everyone who helps you throughout the numerous stages of your journey.

Buses, Subways, and Trains

Any type of travel can test your manners and tolerance level, and a well-mannered traveler is the best kind there is. Whether riding a short distance on a bus or subway, or commuting for hours on a train, being in a closed, confined space can be stressful.

There are many—and frequent—offenses you'll see while traveling on public transportation. Be alert and practice your good transit manners!

liv on traveling

Because of my work, I've had the incredible opportunity of traveling all over the world, getting to experience many different countries and cultures. I've found myself in some pretty interesting and at times funny situations. Though we are all connected now around the world, each culture is unique. When traveling to another country for business or pleasure, I always do a little research about where I'm going. I ask a lot of questions about local customs, holidays, and religions to make myself and the people around me feel more at ease.

DO stand behind the subway safety line when trains are entering and exiting the station.

DO step aside before boarding a train to allow exiting passengers to depart. Rushing to get on board is not only rude but also can cause someone to fall.

DO move as far into the car as possible to make space for others. If you're standing near the door at a stop where others need to exit, briefly step off the train and reenter as soon as they have exited.

DO keep your body language controlled and confined to the space within your own seat.

DO

DO be careful if you're carrying packages, and avoid hitting the people seated as you walk to your seat. Tuck your bag or package underneath your seat close to your legs, or hold it close to your body so it does not disturb anyone else.

DO give up your seat to an older person, a pregnant woman, someone with small children, or someone who is disabled.

DO show your gratitude when riding on a bus. Smile and say hello to the bus driver; when you get off the bus, say, "Thank you."

DO use earphones when listening to music.

Taxi Tact

Be cautious and use only a recognizable taxi company. So-called gypsy taxis are not properly licensed to transport passengers. If your driver knows only a little English, be patient and speak slowly in clear and simple language. In taxis and limousines, the back passenger-side seat is best. When traveling alone, this is the seat you should take, so you may easily exit onto the sidewalk rather than the street. When traveling with an executive, he or she takes the best seat, and you take the seat behind the driver. Be aware that the reverse is true in some countries, such as England.

Here are some tactful tips for taxi riders.

- **If you and another person hail a taxi at the same time, take the high road and let the other person take the taxi. Consider it your good deed for the day.**

- **If you see a taxi a block away and hail it, don't impatiently jump into another one that pulls up first.**

- **Don't run to a taxi that someone else has already hailed. Poor manners!**

- **Don't eat or drink in a taxi. A sudden stop or swerve and you could stain your clothes or the taxi seat.**

- **Don't litter the seat or the floor. Politely ask the driver if he has a trash bag, and if he does, increase your tip and he'll gladly accept and dispose of your trash.**

- Politely tell the driver which side of the street you want to be dropped off on. Open the door and get out only on the curb side. A limousine driver will open the door for you.

- Twenty percent of the fare is appropriate for a tip. If the driver was helpful in carrying bags or other items, increase the tip.

- Speak up immediately if the driver is speeding or driving recklessly, or if the radio volume is too loud. Remember, the driver is providing a service that you will be paying for. His job is to make your ride efficient and comfortable.

Airports and Planes

Today air travel is very casual and impersonal. The huge numbers of air travelers cause stress for airline staff, pilots, crews, and passengers, which can easily turn into anxiety and rudeness. Because good manners aren't used as often as they should be by travelers, the good manners you maintain will be profoundly appreciated.

DO check in online for your boarding pass.

DO have a valid government-issued picture ID.

DO take your seat as quickly as possible.

DO be patient when deplaning.

DON'T make jokes at security.

DON'T bring anything that resembles a weapon.

5

DINING SKILLS

· ·

The world was my oyster,
but I used the wrong fork.

—OSCAR WILDE

Dining at a fine restaurant for business or pleasure can be a delightful experience, once you're no longer frazzled by forks, nervous about napkins, or frightened by formalities.

Practice dining etiquette at home and while eating at restaurants, whether fast food or fancy. Practice until the process is automatic. Then you won't become flustered by details when you need your skills the most.

They don't teach etiquette much anymore, but if
you ever have to choose between Incredibly Advanced
Accounting for Overachievers and Remedial Knife
and Fork, head for the silverware.

—HARVEY MacKAY

The Basics and Beyond

Polishing your table manners won't be intimidating as long as you remember that learning is not a passive activity. The responsibility for results belongs to you. It's a matter of commitment, common sense, homework, and, most important, practice.

Should you forget what to do during the meal, relax. Consider your next logical move as well as what seems the most mannerly, and then do it! In this chapter, the basics are explained along with some special touches that will serve you well in business and social arenas, no matter where you are.

Responding to an Invitation

When you're invited to an event, a casual dinner at someone's home, a company party, or a wedding, your response should be given in the same format in which the invitation was received: by telephone, mail, e-mail, or text. Regardless of whether you accept or decline an invitation, always be polite and respond promptly. If you accept an invitation and then find you're unable to attend, let your host know immediately. (If you find that you're available at the last minute, it's too late to join the event.)

The Savvy Guest

It's your duty to be a thoughtful and appreciative guest. Don't arrive early, but be no more than fifteen minutes late. Use this opportunity to meet new people and improve your skills as a guest. Greet your host first; however, don't take up too much of his or her time. Greet and introduce yourself to the other guests, and resist talking only to those you know.

See Mingling, page 49, and Conversation, page 42.

When you respond to an invitation, the savvy host may ask if there are foods you can't eat (if you have a vegan or gluten-free diet, for example). Let the host know, in a brief manner, if you have any issues with a specific food. (If the host doesn't ask, it's the duty of a guest to inform the host of an allergy.) However, the burden of satisfying those on special diets shouldn't rest entirely on the host, and guests shouldn't expect a host to alter the menu just for them. If you don't eat meat, be content with the vegetables, salad, bread, and dessert (and it's always an option to eat lightly beforehand).

DID YOU KNOW?

The first formal work on table manners was written by a Milanese monk, Bonvicino da Riva, in 1290. One of his bits of advice was: "Do not cross your legs on the laid-out table."

DO thank your host when you're ready to leave, and say good-bye to the other guests.

DO ask and get permission if you wish to bring an uninvited guest, and make sure to ask well before the day of the party.

DO

DO write a thank-you note within twenty-four hours. A handwritten note has greater impact than a text or e-mail. If you normally correspond with your host by text or e-mail, this is fine, and widely acceptable among busy professionals.

DO write a thank-you note to a more formal host not in your peer group: your boss or your grandmother, for example.

BEING A SAVVY GUEST

DON'T act shy and stand or sit in one place.

DON'T make a dash for the bar or food; you were invited for your company, not to satisfy your thirst or hunger.

DON'T

DON'T arrive early, but be no more than fifteen minutes late.

GIFTING THE HOST

Consider the following tips when gifting the host.

- **Always attach a card to the gift so the host will remember who brought it.**

- **Wine is a good host gift; however, don't expect it to be served, as it may not go well with the prepared meal.**

- **Coffee-table books featuring your host's interests are wonderful gifts.**

- **Small gifts or books for children in the house are thoughtful and will be appreciated.**

liv on being a good guest

When someone invites me to his or her home for a dinner party, I like to take the host a bottle of wine or some flowers. After dinner I offer my help with clearing the table or doing dishes. I always appreciate it when someone helps me when I'm the host.

dorothea on being a good guest

It's best to take a potted plant or flowers already arranged in a vase. Avoid arriving with an unarranged bouquet of flowers, as the host will have to find a vase, trim the stems, and arrange the flowers. This unexpected chore, coupled with answering the door and checking on dinner, can be stressful for even the most seasoned host.

When you're a guest of honor, a flower arrangement or potted plant delivered by a florist the day before or the morning of the party is a kind and thoughtful gesture of your appreciation.

I invited a Marine Corps General, his wife, and four other guests to dinner. Before dinner we enjoyed drinks and hors d'oeuvres. We sat down at the table, and my husband delivered a welcome toast and wished everyone *bon appétit.*

Scallops St. Jacques was my first course, and I noticed that the General wasn't eating. "Is something wrong, General?" I asked.

"I can't eat seafood," he replied.

I apologized and said, "May I get you something else?"

"Well, yes, a little bologna and cheese sandwich would make a great first course for me."

I was rather taken aback and not prepared to jump up and make a sandwich that would destroy the flow of my four-course dinner. I reached for his porcelain menu stand and said, "General, please take a peek at my menu. I have three more courses coming."

"Wonderful. Carry on. I'll make brilliant conversation while you folks finish your scallops."

My main course was tenderloin of beef, followed by a salad course with cheese and slices of baguette. Dessert was shortbread cookies and parfaits of strawberries over which I had poured a generous amount of Grand Marnier liqueur. The General just sat and stared at his parfait. My questioning glance brought forth his reply: "Dorothea, yes, I hate to tell you, but I'm also allergic to strawberries."

Smiling, I asked, "General, would you like an ice cream sandwich?"

"Yes, it's my very favorite dessert," he replied.

The General ate his favorite dessert with a fork and spoon. His lively conversation and humor made the evening a great success. After dessert, we moved to the living room and enjoyed chocolates, coffee, and stimulating conversation.

This taught me an invaluable lesson. I learned always to ask, "Is there anything you don't eat?" when I invite guests. I never use the word *allergy,* and I've discovered several friends with food sensitivities who hadn't mentioned them prior to my asking.

Arriving at the Table

When you approach the table, look for place cards, which are used at many business and social luncheons and dinners for more than six guests to help guests locate their seats. Cards are placed either on the center of the napkin, when the napkin is on the service plate, or on the table directly above the service plate. Guests should never rearrange them. If place cards aren't on the table, remain standing and wait for the host to indicate where to sit. When there isn't a host, wait until two or three people have arrived before you sit down. If you arrive at the table and other guests are mingling, approach each new person and introduce yourself, and greet those you already know.

Sitting and Rising

The correct way to sit down or rise from a chair at the table is from the right side of the chair. (The chair's right is determined from the back of the chair.) To sit down, approach your chair from the right and enter it from your left side. To rise, push your chair back from the table, rise and exit from the right side, and push your chair back under the table.

Why from the right side? History accords the place of honor to the right side because most people are right-handed. A man pulls out the chair for the woman on his right, pushes her chair into place, and then seats himself by entering his chair from the right side. It wouldn't make sense for him to dart behind his chair to enter from the left side.

If the tables are placed close together, or it's a banquette against a wall, making it awkward to follow these guidelines, enter and exit the chair or banquette in the most convenient way.

In social situations, men still pull out chairs for women, and this courtesy should be acknowledged with "thank you." However, professional women don't expect male colleagues to hold their chairs at business functions. A savvy man may offer by saying, "May I hold your chair?" A savvy woman will always say, "Thank you." At casual dinners or family meals, women usually seat themselves. For family meals at home or in restaurants, young men can practice being gentlemen by pulling out the chairs for women of all ages.

Excusing Yourself

If for any reason you have to leave the table during a meal, excuse yourself quietly to those present. You don't have to explain why you're leaving, but don't just get up and leave. Place your napkin, loosely folded, on the seat of your chair (see Napkins, page 132).

Tabletop Taboos

Personal items don't belong on the dining table, no matter how casual the meal. No cell phones, PDAs, eyeglasses, eyeglass cases, keys, purses, gloves, or hats. If it isn't part of the meal, it shouldn't be on the table. (Even the most beautiful crystal-studded purse doesn't belong there.) The exception to the rule about personal items is the working meal, where you may sit at the table and work on a project after you've finished eating.

A small evening purse is placed on one's lap, under the napkin, during a meal. A briefcase, laptop, iPad, or large purse should be placed next to you on a banquette seat or a chair. If there isn't a chair or an available seat near you, place a large valuable item next to your feet and maintain contact with it throughout the meal. Never hang a purse on the back of your chair, as it may impede service or tempt theft, even in upscale restaurants.

I was invited to lunch with three attorneys at a conference in Washington, D.C. I noticed one of the men had placed a large briefcase on the floor next to his chair on the right side. The server took our order and later returned with our plates of food on a large tray, which he placed on a stand. He removed a plate from the tray to place on the table, and suddenly the tray and plates of food crashed onto the table. The man's upright briefcase had fallen over and the server tripped on it. Our table was, of course, the center of attention; the waiter was quite embarrassed, and we were as well.

DID YOU KNOW?

At around age sixteen, George Washington transcribed a slim volume of 110 rules under the title "Rules of Civility and Decent Behaviour in Company and Conversation." While these rules are more than 250 years old, they're still relevant in today's business and social arenas. Here are several of Washington's timeless rules.

● If anyone comes to speak to you while you are sitting, stand up, though he be your inferior, and when you present seats, let it be to everyone according to his degree.

● Put not another bite into your mouth till the former be swallowed. Let not your morsels be too big for the jowls.

● Drink not nor talk with your mouth full, neither gaze about you while you are drinking.

Place-Setting Savvy

A place setting at a table is like a road map to your meal. When you're first seated at the table, briefly study the placement of the silverware and glasses. This will help you gain a comfort level. The amount of silverware at a place setting depends on the number of courses to be served.

There's a simple rule to remember about silverware: start on the outside and work your way inward toward the center.

THREE-COURSE PLACE SETTING
Salad, Main Course, Dessert

This place setting indicates the salad course will be eaten first; the main course second; the dessert course third. The fork and spoon placed at the top of the plate are used for dessert.

FIVE-COURSE PLACE SETTING

Soup, Fish Course, Main Course, Salad, Dessert

This formal place setting will help familiarize you with the various utensils used at a multicourse meal. This place setting indicates the soup course will be eaten first; the fish course second; the main course third; the salad course fourth; the dessert course fifth. The fork and spoon placed at the top of the plate are used for dessert.

Note: **The butter spreader may be laid on the bread-and-butter plate in a vertical or horizontal position.**

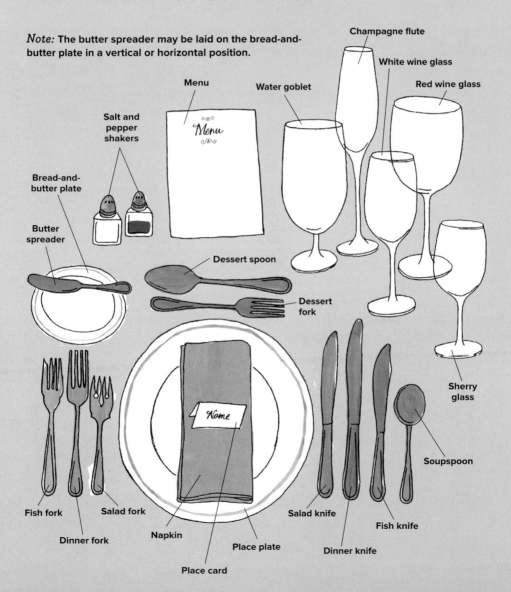

Champagne flute

White wine glass

Red wine glass

Menu

Water goblet

Salt and pepper shakers

Bread-and-butter plate

Butter spreader

Dessert spoon

Dessert fork

Sherry glass

Soupspoon

Fish fork

Salad fork

Salad knife

Fish knife

Dinner fork

Napkin

Place card

Place plate

Dinner knife

DID YOU KNOW?

The development of dining utensils took thousands of years; starting with knives, people in the Near and Far East next invented spoons, chopsticks, and finally forks.

The fork was introduced to the Italians in the eleventh century in Tuscany, brought by a Turkish princess who married a wealthy nobleman from Venice. Forks had been in common use in the royal courts of the Middle East since at least the seventh century, and the princess had eaten with them all her life. The church leaders of Venice were shocked, and condemned their use as an affront to God's intentions for fingers. Thereafter, the fork disappeared from the table for almost three hundred years. It wasn't until the late sixteenth century that the fork gained acceptance in Italy, when upper-class Italians expressed renewed interest in cleanliness.

The French thought it was affected to eat with a fork, and the nobility didn't accept it until the seventeenth century, when court etiquette declared it uncivilized to eat meat with the fingers. It took longer for the fork to gain acceptance in England because it was thought to be a feminine utensil. Thomas Coryate, an English traveler and philosopher who had been to Italy and France, published a book in 1611 that included the Italian custom of eating with a fork. He declared himself the first man in London to eat with a fork.

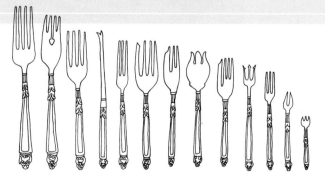

Glassware

Glasses are placed in the order of use, on the right above the soup-spoon and knives. This is logical because the majority of people are right-handed. As you drink from each glass, replace it in approximately the same position at the table.

Refrain from moving glasses to the left side, even if you're left-handed. You would be invading the place setting of the diner on your left.

Should you choose not to drink wine, touch your fingertips lightly to the glass rim as the waiter or sommelier approaches. Never cover the glass with the palm of your hand, or turn your glass upside down.

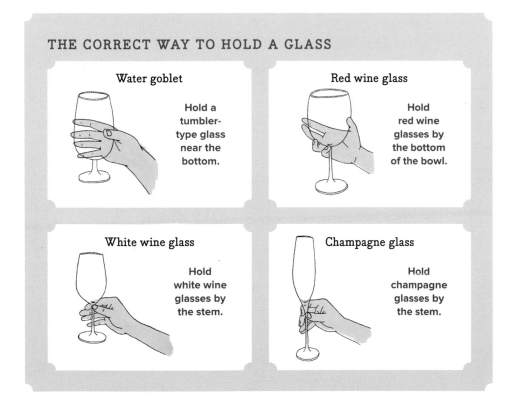

THE CORRECT WAY TO HOLD A GLASS

Water goblet

Hold a tumbler-type glass near the bottom.

Red wine glass

Hold red wine glasses by the bottom of the bowl.

White wine glass

Hold white wine glasses by the stem.

Champagne glass

Hold champagne glasses by the stem.

Napkins

A large simple folded napkin may be placed on the left side of your place setting. (In Europe, the napkin is often placed to the right side of the place setting.) The napkin may also be placed on the service plate if one is used, or on the table in the center of your place setting.

When there's a host, wait until he or she picks up a napkin, then pick up yours and place it on your lap. When there isn't a host, wait until two or three people in your group are seated, then pick up your napkin. A large napkin is folded in half with the fold facing the waistline, while a smaller napkin is opened completely. In many upscale restaurants, a server may drape a napkin on your lap.

If you leave the table during a meal, place your napkin, loosely folded, on the seat of your chair. A napkin is never returned to the table until you're ready to leave; it stays on your lap, even after the meal is finished. When you're ready to leave the table, pick up the napkin by the center, gather it loosely, and place it to the left of the plate. If the plate has been removed, you may place the napkin on the table in front of you.

DID YOU KNOW?

The word *napkin* derives from the old French *napéron,* meaning "little tablecloth." The first napkins were the size of today's bath towels, practical at the time because the multicourse meal was eaten entirely with the fingers. The ancient Egyptians, Greeks, and Romans used them to cleanse the hands and face during a meal, which could last for many hours. At many such meals, it was proper to provide a fresh napkin with each course.

DO

DO pause briefly to see if the server drapes a napkin on your lap.

DO follow the lead of your host and pick up your napkin after the host does.

DO unfold your napkin on your lap.

DO place your napkin on the seat of your chair when you leave the table during a meal.

DON'T

DON'T tuck a napkin under your chin, or into your shirt.

DON'T unfold your napkin above the table.

DON'T blot lipstick on a cloth napkin or use it as a handkerchief.

DON'T place a cloth or paper napkin on your plate after eating.

DON'T place your napkin back on the table while others are still eating.

DON'T crumple a paper napkin.

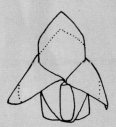

American and European Styles of Eating

There are two styles of eating when using silverware: one is American, the other European, also known as Continental (I will use the term "European style"). Although both are perfectly acceptable, the American style is less efficient and may appear clumsy, due to the zigzag transfer of a utensil between hands and the clatter of a knife constantly hitting the plate as it's placed on the rim. The European style is much more widely used around the world, quieter, more efficient, and more elegant.

The key is knowing how to handle your fork and knife with confidence while eating in the American or European style, and to know where to place them when you finish each course.

· · · · · · · · · · · ·

Eating an artichoke is like getting to know someone really well.

—WILLI HASTINGS

· · · · · · · · · · · ·

DID YOU KNOW?

Europeans were as right-handed with forks as Americans were until about the 1840s. Then the fashionable upper class stopped shifting their forks back and forth. It's possible that as more middle-class eaters learned to convey food into their mouths with tines instead of blades, the upper class hit upon this consistency as a new class identification. The style became fashionable first in England, but in 1853, a French etiquette book advised that those who wished to eat fashionably should not change their fork to their right hand after they cut their meat, but raise it to their mouth in their left hand. The final result? Europeans of all classes began eating this way.

However, the Americans, perhaps out of pioneering pride, refused to change and continued to switch the fork to the right hand before raising it to the mouth. Jokes about the American zigzag eating habit have persisted for more than a hundred years, but many have held to the old style. Today, more Americans are worldwide travelers who have taken to the European style of eating.

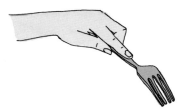

The following description of how to use silverware is for a right-handed person; you may reverse the position if you're left-handed. However, don't rearrange the silverware at the place setting before you start eating.

CUTTING FOOD

Food is cut the same way in both the American and European styles. Hold the knife in your right hand with your index finger on the handle, overlapping the blade no more than 1 inch because you need leverage to cut. Hold the fork, tines down, in your left hand and cut off one bite-sized piece of food; use your knife to push the bite more securely onto the fork. Cut only one piece of food at a time.

PLACEMENT OF KNIFE

After cutting a bite-sized piece, rest the knife on the rim of your plate with the cutting edge of the blade pointing inward, toward the center. Transfer the fork, tines upward, to the right hand and raise the speared food to your mouth. The fork is steadied between the index finger and the middle finger, and secured by the thumb as shown.

HANDS DURING THE MEAL

Americans have traditionally been taught to rest their hands on their lap when not actively cutting and eating. When eating in the American style, keep your free hand on your lap, or rest your wrist on the edge of the table but never your elbows or forearms.

REST POSITION

If you need to use a napkin or pick up a glass before you finish a course, do the following to rest your silverware on your plate: Visualize a clock face. Place your knife on the upper right rim of the plate, the tip at 11:00 and the handle at 2:00. The cutting edge of the blade points inward toward the center. Place your fork on the right side of the plate with the handle on the lower right side, at approximately 4:00, and the tines up, pointing to 10:00.

FINISHED POSITION

Fork and Knife

When you finish eating, place the handles of the knife and fork at 4:00 on the plate. The tip of the knife and the tines of the fork point to 10:00 on the plate. The tines of the fork are turned up, and the knife blade always faces the fork.

Fork Only

When you're eating only with a fork, place it tines up on the plate in the 10:20 finished position. If a knife was provided, remove it from the table and place it on your plate in the finished position as described at left.

Note: The finished position is a signal to the server that you've finished the course. The position makes it easier for the server to safely and easily remove the plate and silverware from the right side of the diner. Lefties may reverse silverware while eating, but always place it as shown when finished with each course and when finished with the meal.

The following description of how to use silverware is for a right-handed person; you may reverse the position if you're left-handed. However, don't rearrange silverware at the place setting before you start eating.

CUTTING FOOD

Food is cut the same way in both the American and European styles. Hold the knife in your right hand with your index finger on the handle, overlapping the blade no more than 1 inch because you need leverage to cut. Hold the fork, tines down, in your left hand and cut off one bite-sized piece of food; use your knife to push the bite more securely onto the fork. Cut only one piece of food at a time.

FORK TO MOUTH

With the fork still in your left hand, lift your fork, tines down, to your mouth by twisting your wrist and raising your forearm slightly. Keep the knife in your right hand. You may use the knife to push a small amount of vegetable onto the tines of the fork with the meat. When not cutting, keep the knife low or rest it on the edge of the plate; don't gesture with it while talking.

Throughout Europe and England, you will see diners using a knife to steady or push food onto the fork, even when the food doesn't require cutting. (Yes, even salad!)

HANDS DURING THE MEAL

When eating in the European style, both hands should always be visible, never placed on the lap. (This custom dates to ancient times, when the fear of a concealed weapon was no laughing matter.) Wrists are placed on the edge of the table but never the elbows or forearms.

REST POSITION

This position is used when you're pausing between bites, to use your napkin, or to pick up a glass. Think of it as an inverted V. Cross the fork and knife on your plate, with the fork tines down, over the knife. The tip of the fork faces 2:00 on the plate clock, and the handle faces 8:00. The knife tip faces 10:00 and the handle faces 4:00. The cutting edge of the knife blade always faces inward.

FINISHED POSITION

When you finish eating, place the handles of the knife and fork at 4:00 on the plate. The tip of the knife and the tines of the fork point to 10:00 on the plate. The tines of the fork are turned up, and the cutting edge of the knife blade always faces inward toward the fork.

Note: The European and American finished positions are the same.

ENGLISH FINISHED POSITION

The English fork and knife placement varies from the European finished position by the placement of the tips of the knife and fork at 12:00 and the handles at 6:00. The cutting edge of the knife blade faces inward and the fork tines are turned down.

EATING DESSERT—AMERICAN AND EUROPEAN STYLES

When two eating utensils are presented together, such as a fork and spoon, the fork is used to steady the portion, and the spoon to cut and convey the bite to the mouth. The fork and dessert spoon are positioned as shown in the illustration, below left. First, transfer the dessert utensils from above the plate to the sides of the plate (below center). To steady the dessert portion, the fork is held in the left hand, tines down. The dessert spoon is held in the right hand to cut and convey a bite to the mouth (see the above illustration). The finished position is 10:20, with the spoon to the right of the fork, fork tines up (below right).

If the dessert is ice cream or pudding, use a spoon. In this case, only a spoon will be placed above the plate.

Note: When only a fork is provided for dessert, place it tines up on the plate in the 10:20 finished position. This position also applies when only a spoon is provided for dessert.

dorothea on posing as an exotic vegetable consultant

Revealing one's profession as an Etiquette and Protocol Consultant before sitting down to a meal can cause your intended dining companion to either disappear or politely say, "Oh, my. I see Mark across the room and I promised to sit with him." It happened to me so many times I created a new identity for myself—I became a consultant on "exotic vegetables."

During the mingling time prior to sitting down to lunch, I would often meet a new person and draw him or her into conversation. When someone asked me, "What line of work are you in, Dorothea?" I replied, "Well, I'm a consultant on exotic vegetables." Then I would hear, "What does that mean?" Next I would go into explicit detail about exotic new vegetables on the market and how I was under contract to dozens of upscale restaurants all over the country to keep them updated about the latest exotic vegetables, where they're grown and the suppliers' contact information.

At one luncheon, I met the CEO of a corporation who was also a "foodie" with a passion for cooking and experimenting with recipes. He said, "Let's sit together. I want to hear more about those exotic vegetables." When lunch was served, there on the plate next to the breast of chicken was an array of tiny squash and zucchini. He looked at me and said, "What are those? I've never seen those before."

"Those are exotic vegetables," I replied.

Well, he loved them. As the meal drew to a close, he sensed that my whole act was a put-on. He turned to me and politely said, "Tell me, what do you really do?"

"Well, since you asked so politely, I'll tell you. I'm an Etiquette and Protocol Consultant."

"Ouch, I'm glad you told me now since we've finished eating. How did I do?"

"A-plus," I replied. We parted friends and soon I was hired as the corporation's Etiquette and Protocol Consultant.

SALAD

The salad course may be eaten with the salad fork and knife. Leave the knife on the table if the salad can be eaten with the fork alone. However, you may use your knife to cut a large leaf into bite-sized pieces. Place both the fork and the knife in the "finished" position when you're done, even if you've used only the fork. When the salad is not set in front of you as a separate course, the salad plate will be on your left, and the bread-and-butter plate above it.

Buffet Style

Buffet meals are very popular today. This relaxed serving style can accommodate a flexible number of guests.

OPEN OR UNASSIGNED SEATING

- It's difficult to serve yourself and hold a beverage and a plate while navigating the buffet line. Look around or ask where to desposit used glasses.

- Pick up a plate, a napkin, and silverware.

- Avoid the temptation to overload your plate; you may return for additional helpings.

- Carry your plate to the space designated by the host.

- Look for a chair that has a table near it to hold a beverage if you choose to get one. Be prepared to spread your napkin on your lap and balance your plate on it.

- Politely join in the conversation with others in the room, and introduce yourself to those you haven't met before.

- When you've finished eating, look for a service table to leave used plates. Offer to take someone else's plate as well.

SEATED BUFFETS

- If the event is a large seated buffet, there may be a seating chart that will indicate at which table you will be seated. Or, "you are seated at" (YASA) cards may be given to assist guests in finding their tables.

- At your table, look for a place card with your name.

- At a seated buffet, the table will be set with napkins, silverware, and beverage glasses.

- If there isn't a seating chart or place cards, you may choose an available table and deposit your beverage. After you've selected your food, carry your plate to the table and be seated.

- Introduce yourself to everyone you haven't met before.

- Waitstaff will service the table.

DESSERT AND BEVERAGES

At an open buffet, coffee cups, water/wine glasses, and other beverage glasses are usually placed next to self-service stations for guests to help themselves. Desserts for both open and seated buffets will be placed on a table with plates and forks and spoons.

During the Meal

Whether you're eating while seated at a table or balancing a plate on your lap, the key is to be polite, act as if you belong, and let the conversation flow.

Once you're seated, introduce yourself to the person on both your right and your left. Try to find something to talk about that is interesting and inclusive; the key to a good conversation is in hearing the other person's point of view rather than expressing your own. If the table isn't large, include the other diners around you, because it's easier for three or four people to join in a single conversation. If you're seated between two diners, talk to each one and even include those on the opposite side of the table if the table isn't large. You don't want to shout across the table.

DO

DO be mindful of your posture: sit up straight and keep your arms off the table.

DO use your knife and fork quietly; avoid loud clatter against your plate.

DO take small bites, and you'll find it's easier to join the conversation.

DO discreetly remove an object such as a bone or gristle from your mouth with your thumb and index finger, and place it on the rim of your plate. Camouflage it with bits of food if too unsightly.

DO time your eating so that you finish about the same time as everyone else.

DO take care of personal grooming, such as applying lipstick or removing food caught in your teeth, in the restroom.

DON'T

DON'T talk with your mouth full of food, or chew with your mouth open.

DON'T overload your plate at buffets, or overload your fork when you eat.

DON'T gesture with a fork or knife in your hand when you're not using it; place it in the rest position on your plate.

DON'T tip up the glass or cup too much when drinking; keep each one at a slight angle.

DON'T push a plate away from you when you're finished eating. Leave it where it is with the silverware correctly placed in the finished position.

· · · · · · · · · · · · · ·

DON'T
text at the table.

DON'T
butter the whole
roll; break off one
bite-sized portion, then
butter and eat it.

DON'T
tuck your napkin
into your shirt
collar like a bib.

DON'T
flip your tie
over your
shoulder.

Eating with Chopsticks

The use of chopsticks isn't complicated; it simply requires practice. This easy guide will give you the skills to eat sushi, sashimi, or stir-fry. These instructions are for a right-handed person; reverse them if you're left-handed.

DO turn the chopsticks around and use the handle ends to place food from the communal platter onto your plate, then reverse the chopsticks and eat.

DO pick up sushi with the chopsticks by gently gripping the sushi lengthwise, so the rice doesn't fall apart. Dip one end of the sushi, rice side down, into the soy sauce, then place the whole piece in your mouth with the soy-dipped end first and the fish side down on your tongue. You may also eat sushi with your fingers. Pick it up gently, using your thumb and middle finger, then proceed as if you're using chopsticks.

DO bite an extra large piece in half, dip the uneaten portion in the dipping sauce, then eat.

DO place chopsticks side by side on the chopstick rest when not in use, or rest them side by side on your plate if a rest is not provided.

DON'T stand chopsticks in a bowl of rice. This signals an offering to the deceased in East Asian cultures.

DON'T cross chopsticks. This is a symbol of death in the Chinese culture.

DON'T point or gesture with your chopsticks.

DON'T lick your chopsticks.

Note: Chopstick etiquette varies in Asian countries. These guidelines are the most popular and universally accepted.

EXERCISE
Practice using chopsticks by picking up popcorn, grapes, cubes of cheese, carrot strips, or bite-sized pieces of apple.

1 Rest one chopstick on the base between your thumb and index finger.

2 Rest the chopstick on the pad of your ring finger to steady it. This chopstick should remain stationary while you're eating.

3 Hold the second chopstick between your thumb and index finger, resting it on the pad of your middle finger. It should be parallel to the first chopstick. The narrow tips of both chopsticks must be even to help you pinch the food.

4 Use the top chopstick as a lever. The bottom chopstick remains stationary, serving as a base on which to clamp the food. Don't cross the broad ends of the chopsticks as this will make it difficult to pick up food.

5 Pick up food at an angle for stability.

How to Eat Various Foods

Artichokes: Eat with your fingers. Remove each leaf, dip the soft end in sauce, and then pull it through your teeth to remove the edible portion. Discard the remainder of the leaves on the side of your plate. Secure the heart with a fork and scrape away the thistle with a knife. Cut the heart into bite-sized pieces and dip in the sauce.

Asparagus: Cut into bite-sized portions and eat with a fork. In Europe it's eaten with the fingers provided the spears are not too long.

Bacon: Eat with a knife and fork. Very crisp bacon may be picked up with your fingers.

Beverages—coffee and tea: Fill the cup only one-half to three-quarters full. Milk, cream, sugar, or lemon is added after, never before, the beverage is poured. A cup is held with the index finger through the handle, with the thumb just above and the second finger below the handle for support. Never lift the little finger in the air, because it's an affectation. Don't cradle the cup in one or both hands. Never place a wet spoon on the table. Place it on the saucer or on a plate.

When a tea bag is served with a cup of hot water, allow the tea to steep until it reaches the strength you prefer. Request an extra saucer to hold the tea bag. Don't place it on your saucer; it will drain and you will end up with a dripping cup. Never drain a tea bag by winding the string around a spoon. Fold the tea bag wrapper and place it next to the saucer holding the teapot. If you simply can't bear to look at it, fold it and slide it under the saucer holding the teapot, or under the saucer holding your cup.

Request a saucer for disposable sugar wrappers and milk containers.

Bread: Place the bread or roll on your bread plate and break off one bite-sized portion, then butter and eat it. Don't pull the roll in half, then cover it with butter.

When bread is served in a basket, the person nearest the basket starts. If you start, or when the basket comes to you, take some bread and pass the basket to the person on your right.

Butter: When butter is passed, take a portion onto your bread plate with the butter server. If pats are used, pick them up with the serving fork and place on your plate. If a butter server or fork isn't provided, use your butter spreader.

Cake: If served in small portions and not sticky, it may be eaten with your fingers. Otherwise use a fork. If served with ice cream, use a fork and spoon (see page 140).

Caviar: If you're seated, take a spoonful of caviar and place it on your bread plate. Using your butter spreader, spread it onto toast. If it's served with small pancakes (blini) and sour cream, use a knife and fork. If you're standing, spread caviar on toast with a knife and pick it up with your fingers.

Cheese: From a cheese tray, cut a slice and place it on your plate. Hard cheese is placed on either a cracker or bread and eaten with the fingers or a fork. Use your knife to spread a soft cheese on a cracker or bread and eat it with your fingers.

Chicken, duck, and turkey are eaten with a knife and fork. Fried chicken may be eaten with your fingers at a casual gathering.

Condiments (ketchup, mustard, relish, preserves, jelly, jam, etc.): At a seated meal, a condiment is best served in a small dish with a serving utensil, and put on your plate alongside, not on, your food. Dip a forkful of food at a time, or you may put the condiment on the food with your knife.

Cookies that are too large to eat in two or three bites should be broken into bite-sized pieces.

Corn on the cob is served only at casual meals. Butter and season several rows at a time, not the whole ear. Hold the ear firmly with the fingers of both hands.

Doughnuts: Don't dunk them in public. If the setting is casual, go ahead.

Eggs: Hard-cooked eggs are eaten with a fork. Soft-cooked eggs served in an eggcup can be eaten out of the shell. Slice off the top of the shell with a knife, and eat the egg with a spoon. Soft-cooked eggs can also be scooped out of the shell into a small dish and eaten with a spoon.

Escargot: Hold the shell in tongs and use a snail fork held in the other hand to remove the snail from its shell. Dip small pieces of bread into the garlic butter with the snail fork.

Fish: It's rare to be served a whole fish in America. However, in many countries, small fish are served complete with the heads and tails.

Hold the fish fork in your left hand and the fish knife in your right hand and bone as follows: secure the fish with your fork and use your knife to cut off the head and tail and place them to one side of the plate; cut away the small edging of the fish all along the stomach, to remove the small bones; repeat along the backbone, and lift away the top fillet. The backbone will then be exposed and the fillet will be free of bones. After eating it, slip the knife between the other fillet and the backbone. Lift away the backbone and put it next to the head and tail.

If tiny bones get in your mouth, remove them with your thumb and forefinger and place them on the rim of your plate.

If served a filleted fish, you may use only the fish fork. If you're eating only with the fork, leave the knife on the table until you finish the course.

When squeezing lemon over fish, hold the wedge in your right hand while squeezing it over the fish. To keep the juice from spraying, use your left hand as a shield.

Fries are halved and eaten with a fork. In casual settings, you may use your fingers.

Garnishes: Decorative greens and fruit or vegetable garnishes are eaten with a fork.

Ice cream: Unless it's in a cone, eat it with a spoon. When it's served as Baked Alaska, use a fork and spoon.

Lemon: Secure a wedge with a fork and press out the juice with your other hand. Your hand also serves as a shield.

Lobsters: The claws are cracked with a nutcracker. The meat is extracted with a seafood fork and dipped in butter or sauce. Large pieces are cut into bite-sized pieces and eaten with a fork. The small claws are pulled off and sucked as through a straw. Stuffed lobster is eaten with a fork and knife.

Oysters, clams, and mussels on the half-shell: Hold or steady the shell if necessary with one hand and remove the morsel whole with an oyster or cocktail fork. Dip it in the sauce, and eat in one bite.

Pasta: To eat spaghetti, use a fork and separate a few strands. Hold the tip of the prongs against the plate and twirl the fork around to gather the strands onto it. Italians frown on twirling spaghetti strands in a spoon, and cutting the strands up into sections is never done. Small pasta such as tortellini or penne is eaten with a fork. Layered dishes like lasagna, or dishes with stringy cheese, are cut into bite-sized pieces using a fork and knife.

Pie: Firm desserts and crusts can be cut with your fork. If served with ice cream, secure the dessert with your fork, and eat it with the spoon (see page 140).

Pizza is cut into wedges with a knife or pizza cutter. Use your fingers to pick up the wider end of the wedge. You may also fold the pizza in the center lengthwise to keep edges curved inward, which prevents the toppings from dripping. Pizza may also be cut into bite-sized pieces.

Potatoes (baked): Eat with a fork. Butter is added by taking some from your bread plate with the dinner fork. Don't mash potatoes on your plate.

Salad served in bite-sized pieces is eaten with a fork. Wedges and large sections may be cut with a knife. Salad served as a separate course may be eaten with a knife and fork. Use your knife to push lettuce securely onto the tines of the fork.

Salt should be used only after tasting the food. If you are sharing a dish family-style, season only your own portion.

Sandwiches: Tea-type sandwiches and canapés are eaten with your fingers. Club sandwiches may be eaten with a knife and fork or cut into fourths and eaten with your fingers. Open-faced sandwiches are eaten with a knife and fork.

Sauces may be poured or spooned over or beside meat on your plate. A forkful of food at a time may be dipped into the sauce.

Shish kebab: Hold the top of the skewer over your plate with one hand. Then, with a fork held in the other hand, starting at the lower end, carefully push each piece of meat and vegetable onto your plate.

Shrimp cocktail, when the tail is removed, is eaten with a seafood fork—eat large shrimp in two bites. Shrimp with tails may be held by the tail with fingers, dipped in sauce, bitten off, and the tail discarded on the plate underneath the cocktail dish.

Soup is spooned away from you toward the center of a shallow soup plate, soup bowl, or cup. Sip a clear soup from the side of the spoon. Hearty soups containing vegetables and meat may be eaten from the front of the spoon. The soup plate, bowl, or cup may be tipped away from you to fill the spoon with the last sips of soup. When you have finished, place the spoon on the soup plate in the 10:20 clock position. If the soup is served in a soup bowl or cup, place the spoon on the right side of the plate beside the bowl between sips and when you're finished. (In Japan, you may hold your soup bowl in both hands and sip from the rim.)

Sushi and sashimi are picked up with chopsticks or your fingers and eaten whole. If the piece is too large for one bite, you may bite it in half. At a sushi bar, larger pieces may be handed to you and are finger food. When serving yourself from a communal platter,

turn your chopsticks around and use the handle ends to pick up your portions. (See Eating with Chopsticks, page 148.)

Taco: A taco (hard shell) is held in the hand or on the plate while you add the filling and is picked up with both hands. Use a fork to eat filling that may fall out of the taco.

Tortillas: A tortilla (soft-shell) is placed flat on one hand or a plate while you add filling. Fill, roll up, and eat from the end. Eat filling that may fall out of the tortilla with a fork.

Water: Blot your mouth before taking a drink. Don't drink water while food is in your mouth, roll water around your mouth, or swallow loudly. Hold a tumbler-type glass near the bottom, a stemmed glass by the stem, and large goblets at the bottom of the bowl.

Dining Etiquette Recap

Because dining skills are so important, here is a summary of key rules to remember.

DO

DO lean forward slightly and bring your food up to your mouth rather than bring your head down to your food or drink.

DO blot your lips with your napkin and wait until you've swallowed the food in your mouth before taking a sip of your beverage.

DO put butter on your bread plate, not directly onto the roll.

DO break off a bite-sized portion of bread or roll over the bread and butter plate. Hold the bread on the plate while you butter it.

DO look into, not over, the cup or glass when drinking.

DO push food onto your fork with your knife, not your fingers or a piece of bread.

DO leave dropped silver on the floor in a restaurant, and quietly signal the server to bring another piece. In a home, pick up the next piece of silver on the table and continue. If there isn't another utensil, quietly let your host know.

DO point out to your server stones, a bug, or hair in your food, but do so in a calm manner. You'll get a replacement immediately.

DO remember, when the salad is not set in front of you as a separate course, the salad plate will be on your lower left, and the bread-and-butter plate above it. Beverages will be on your right.

DO try a little of everything served to you unless you know you're allergic to a certain food.

DO place your napkin on the seat of your chair if you leave the table briefly. (See Napkins, page 132.)

DON'T

DON'T rearrange silverware or glassware at your place setting.

DON'T salt or season your food before you taste it, especially if you're in someone's home and the cook is sitting at the table.

DON'T cut meat with a knife in a back-and-forth motion, but stroke the knife toward you.

DON'T eat the bread or salad of the person who is seated to your right.

DON'T place any personal items on the table, including your cell phone. (See Tabletop Taboos, page 126.)

DON'T do any personal grooming at the table, such as touching your hair or applying lipstick.

DON'T reach across the table or across another person to get something; if it's out of reach, ask the closest person to pass it to you.

DON'T cut up a whole plateful of food into bite-sized portions before eating.

DON'T place used silverware on the table. A used piece never touches the table again, but is always placed on the plate.

DON'T push your plate away from you when you're finished, lean back from the table, or announce, "I'm full" or "I'm stuffed."

DON'T take pills or other medicines at the table.

— **6** —

THE SAVVY HOST

· ·

A host is like a general:
It takes a mishap to reveal his genius.
—HORACE

In today's global economy, fluently combining business and eating is one of the most effective ways for a rising executive to move up the ranks even faster. You've reached a level where you're trusted to set the tone, and a meal is where all of your social skills come together—your table manners, your ability as a host, your ability to speak well, and your ability to handle others. Never minimize the value of sitting down over a meal to work out a business deal, or to build a relationship prior to discussing business.

Hosting a Business Meal in a Restaurant

Regardless of your gender, when you're the host it's your duty to extend the invitation, make the reservation, and pay the check. The logical business meal is lunch. It's best to extend a business dinner invitation when you know someone, have a set agenda, and have a good reason to meet after six o'clock.

Choose a restaurant where you're known by the staff, one you trust and where you're comfortable. If you use a new restaurant, stop by before your scheduled lunch or dinner to introduce yourself to the maître d' or captain, select a table, and familiarize yourself with the menu and the surroundings.

Be sure the restaurant complements your guest's taste: a low-key person may not be comfortable in an upscale restaurant. However, someone who has entertained you in an upscale restaurant deserves similar treatment.

dorothea on honoring a guest's wish

In the late 1980s, I was asked by a client from China if we could eat at McDonald's because he had heard so much about it. I had planned to take him to the Ritz-Carlton; however, he wanted to observe the operation because he was sure McDonald's would be in China one day. Our McDonald's dinner was a huge hit and so was my business relationship with him. When McDonald's established operations in China, he emerged as a major franchisee. Little did I know how much he had invested in that dinner.

Handling the Check

Arrive fifteen to thirty minutes before your guest. Before you go to your table, affirm with the maître d' and waitstaff that you're the host. Ask the maître d' to imprint your credit card and request that the check be held at his station for your signature, or you may choose to sign the check in advance and request that your standard tip be added. This advance preparation prevents the check from being brought to you at the table. Your receipt will be handed to you discreetly as you leave the restaurant.

Waiting at Your Table

When you go to the table to wait for your guest, ask the maître d' to show your guest to your table. Don't order a drink or open your napkin: you want your guest to think you just sat down. Stand as your guest approaches, regardless of your or the guest's gender, and remain standing until your guest is seated. If you have two guests, put the second across the table from you and the first to your right. If you're hosting several guests, the most important one is seated to your right; the second most important one is seated to your left. A cohost is seated at the opposite end of the table, and the third most important guest is seated on the cohost's right. This seating arrangement works well for business meals.

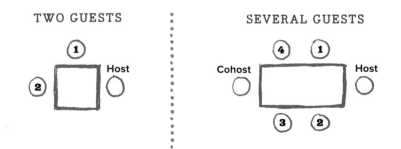

TWO GUESTS

SEVERAL GUESTS

When You Walk in Together

When you greet your guest near the entrance of the restaurant and walk in together, pause at the maître d's station and allow him to lead you to your table. Let the guest follow the maître d' to your table, and you follow the guest. The guest is seated first, in the best seat, which is the first one pulled out from the table, facing out into the room. The ranking guest gets the prime seat, the seat on your right. If there's more than one guest, indicate everyone's places and wait until they're seated before you sit. Follow the seating guidelines on page 159.

Ordering Beverages

Offer your guest a beverage, even if you don't want one, and let your guest decide whether or not to drink alcohol. Order a beverage if your guest does, but it doesn't have to be alcohol; no explanation is necessary.

Ordering the Meal

Make small talk for a few minutes before requesting a menu; this gives you and your guest a chance to relax and connect. Discuss the menu with the server, then put your guest at ease by suggesting one or two items on the menu. Allow your guest to order first. If the guest orders an appetizer and an expensive main course, you should order similar items, though not the same ones. For guests, whether at a neighborhood bistro or a four-star restaurant, it's only fair and considerate to be mindful of costs when making menu choices. At many upscale restaurants, only the host receives a menu with prices. Guests should be discreet when making a selection.

During the Meal

After the orders are taken, move the conversation toward your business agenda. Don't wait until dessert because it shows a lack of respect for the guest's time. It's also your duty to stick to the agenda and control the conversation, especially when you have more than one guest. Discuss only one or two items. Listen and ask questions when necessary.

Be candid if you can't answer a specific question: "I'll check my resources and e-mail you the answer as soon as I return to the office." Never say, "I don't know."

Encourage your guest to have dessert when the server returns with the dessert menu. If your guest orders dessert, you should do the same. The same rule applies if your guest declines dessert but chooses coffee.

liv on conversations during dinner

Sitting with new people at a dinner party, trying to mingle with strangers or new business acquaintances, can be a little like standing alone in the desert. (In my mind, I hear the music from an old western and see a single tumbleweed rolling by.) I often feel a bit shy, and starting a conversation can be tricky at first. Over the years I have learned from practice that a great conversation starter is to ask questions. I find simple conversation is best, especially with someone not so talkative. When the conversation is going well you can usually see it in the person's eyes—they will light up and sparkle when you speak of something that's of interest.

liv on a dining accident

When I was seven years old, my grandparents took me to a new Mexican restaurant. At the end of the meal, the busy waiter returned to our table in a rush with our dessert order. When he suddenly lost control of the tray resting on his shoulder, three orders of fried ice cream came crashing down on top of my head. I was shocked and stunned, to say the least.

I remember how well my grandmother dealt with this situation; she took charge but remained calm in such an elegant way. As tears started to well, she looked me in the eye and said, "Livvy, you're okay." Then she turned to the waiter and said, "It's okay, it was an accident." He was freaking out and kept apologizing over and over again. My grandmother repeated, "It was an accident. Accidents happen," and she even thanked him for helping us clean up the mess and my head.

I thought her graciousness was very important. People can sometimes be very rude when a waiter makes a mistake in a restaurant. In the moment I felt embarrassed and a little bit scared, but at the same time I could empathize with how terrible he must have felt.

When dining accidents happen to me now, I remember the lesson of the fried-ice-cream-on-the-head!

Paying the Check

The host rule is clear: regardless of gender, the person who does the inviting pays the check. Never involve your guest in paying the check. The host requests the check when dessert and coffee are served, if prior arrangements haven't been made. The guest shouldn't take notice of the check, but always thanks the host when saying good-bye.

See Handling the Check, page 159, and When a Group Splits the Check, below.

Closing the Meal

Respect your guest's time and bring the meal to a close. Avoid lingering and discussing topics unrelated to your agenda. Walk your guest to the door, shake hands, and say, "Thank you for the meeting." Follow through on promises when you return to your office.

The No-Host Meal
When a Group Splits the Check

When there isn't a host and several people are expected to share a dinner check, the intentions should be clear when planning the get-together. Hearing "Let's split the check" at the last minute can be embarrassing, so make sure everyone knows what to expect. Remember to take cash, as it makes the process of splitting the bill less painful for the diners and the servers. If someone has ordered frugally or did not consume an alcoholic beverage, then she or he should pay less. It's easier to just take a guess at what the division should be rather than calculate to the penny.

A Wine-Wise Host

Even if you're not a wine expert, knowing the basics will help you project confidence when you're hosting a business meal or entertaining at home. You should feel comfortable asking the sommelier (wine steward) or server for advice on a good choice in keeping with your meal selections.

The bottle will be brought to the table unopened for you to inspect and verify that this is your choice. In some restaurants, wine stewards still offer the opened cork to the host to smell and touch for excess moisture. A moldy or "corky" smell would indicate that the bottle has been improperly stored. When a sample is poured into your glass, sniff the aroma and then take a small sip to measure the quality. Swirling of the wine is done to intensify the aromas: to avoid spilling, place the glass on the table and move it in small circles three to five times. When you approve the selection, wine is poured for your guests, starting with your guest of honor. You are served last.

WINE TIPS FOR THE HOST AT HOME

● Chill white wines and Beaujolais thoroughly, about three to four hours or to 40 to 50 degrees Fahrenheit, before serving. Wines that are fruity and sweet should be chilled to a lower temperature. White wines may be recorked and refrigerated before serving.

● Pour red wines when their temperature is not less than 65 degrees Fahrenheit, or at room temperature. Uncork and allow the wine to breathe one hour before serving. Once opened, don't recork at the table.

● Fill wine glasses half to two-thirds full.

● Pour wine from the guest's right.

● The best wine glass is one that holds 9 to 12 ounces, and has a shape that cups slightly inward at the rim to capture the wine's aroma.

DO touch your fingertips lightly to the glass rim to indicate you don't want wine.

DON'T turn the glass over if you don't want wine.

DON'T cover the glass with the palm of your hand.

Note: **If one *does* want wine, the hand would *not* go near the glass.**

Toasting

Toasting can bring a festive tone to a professional, social, casual, or formal meal and turn it into a special occasion. These basic guidelines for toasting may be used for any occasion/celebration.

THE WELCOME TOAST

The host may propose a toast to welcome guests at the beginning of the meal: "It's a pleasure to have all of you here to share good company and good food. Welcome."

This toast is not directed at an individual person but is meant for everyone. The toast to a guest of honor is offered after dessert has been served.

THE HOST PROPOSES A TOAST TO THE GUEST OF HONOR

To get the attention of a group, stand and hold your glass in the air (don't tap your glass with a piece of silverware). Then put your glass down and talk clearly, slowly, and sincerely about the person you're toasting. Face the person and make eye contact.

As you finish your toast, sweep the room once with your eyes to include the audience, and then look back at the person you're toasting. Pick up your glass, raise it, and say, "Please join me in a toast to [honoree]." Take a sip and sit down.

•   •

DO stand and propose a toast to the guest of honor.

DON'T read your toast. If it's too long to remember, toss it!

DO keep the toast short and simple. Use the three B's: Begin— Be Brief—Be Seated.

DON'T roast the person you're toasting.

THE GUEST OF HONOR

If you are the guest of honor, remain seated during the toast. Don't touch your glass, because when you do, there's a tendency to lift it and drink. Smile, pause briefly, then stand and respond with a toast to the host. Always respond, even if you're not drinking alcohol; water will do fine. Face your host and thank him for his kind welcoming words. As you finish your toast, sweep the room once with your eyes to include the audience. Then look back and face your host, make eye contact, raise your glass in a toast, and take a sip.

Note: Other guests may offer toasts now. Small gatherings of people (two or four) can remain seated and gently clink glasses. It depends on the occasion.

DO follow your host's lead and stand to respond to a toast if your host stood.

DON'T drink a toast to yourself when someone proposes a toast to you. It's as if you're applauding yourself.

DID YOU KNOW?

The custom of a host drinking to a friend's health originated with the Greeks as early as the sixth century B.C.

Spiking decanted wine with poison was a preferred way to dispose of a rival. A host would take the first sip of wine to assure the guests of its safety. This custom of guests following the host in drinking came to represent friendship and goodwill.

The Romans adopted the Greek fondness for poisoning and the custom of drinking as a pledge of friendship. The Roman custom of dropping a burnt piece of toast into a cup of wine is the origin of the verbal usage.

Tipping
(aka Gratuities)

A tip is supposed to be a reward for services performed, as well as a supplement to an employee's income. The word *tip* comes from the mid-eighteenth-century innkeepers' sign **TO INSURE PROMPTNESS.** Patrons deposited a few coins on the table before ordering a meal or drinks and were served faster.

The average tip is 15 to 20 percent of the total bill *before taxes*. A slightly larger tip may be in order if the food and service were outstanding. Some restaurants include a 15 to 20 percent service charge in the European manner, especially if the party is six or more.

The following guide to tips is an average. Remember that tips vary in different communities and, of course, countries.

UPSCALE RESTAURANT

CAPTAIN/HEAD SERVER/ MAÎTRE D'
$10 for special services.

SOMMELIER (WINE STEWARD)
15 percent of the cost of the wine.

SERVER
15 to 20 percent of the bill before tax.

MIDRANGE RESTAURANT/DELI

LUNCH COUNTER
10 to 15 percent of the bill.

BUFFET MEAL
10 percent for the person who serves your table.

VARIOUS SERVICES

FOOD DELIVERIES
10 percent or less of the bill.

PIZZA DELIVERY
$2 for an order totaling $20. A tip for a larger order may be between $3 and $5, depending on the size of the order.

GROCERY STORE DELIVERY
$2 for a small delivery of one or two regular-size bags; $5 for three or more bags.

BELLHOP OR SKYCAP
$2 per bag. For a heavy bag, tip $3. For several bags, tip $5.

COATROOM ATTENDANT

$2 for each coat; increase the tip if you leave a briefcase, a laptop, an umbrella, or a package.

GARAGE ATTENDANT

$3 when your car is brought to the front of the restaurant or hotel; $5 if the attendant helps with doors, packages, and so on.

HOUSEKEEPER IN A HOTEL

Tip $2 for each night. Add an additional tip if you request an extra service. Ask for the name of the housekeeper and place your tip in an envelope addressed to him or her with a personal thank-you note. You may hand the housekeeper the envelope, or leave it at the front desk at checkout.

Note: Housekeeper (not *maid*) is now the preferred term for a person who cleans rooms.

NEWSPAPER DELIVERIES

$20 to $25 once a year at Christmas is appropriate.

RESTROOM ATTENDANT

$1 for each visit. Increase for special service, such as cleaning a spot on your clothing.

TAXI

Meter systems, 15 percent; for long rides, 15 to 20 percent.

BEAUTY SALON/DAY SPA OR BARBERSHOP

SHAMPOO PERSON

$1 to $5, depending on assistance relating to services such as perm and color.

STYLIST

15 to 20 percent.

HAIRCUT AT A BARBERSHOP

15 to 20 percent of the bill.

MAKEUP ARTIST/ AESTHETICIAN

15 to 20 percent of the bill.

NAIL TECHNICIAN

15 to 20 percent of the bill.

MASSAGE THERAPIST

15 to 20 percent of the bill.

Note: If the beauty salon/day spa or barbershop owner provides one of the above services to you, he or she should be tipped. The old rule that one doesn't tip the owner is obsolete. Be mindful that customers should tip for services performed.

a final word

Times change. Manners change. However, the need to have good manners never changes. Good manners are one of the most important keys to success in the business arena. From the recent college graduate hired by a small enterprise to the CEO of a Fortune 500 company, everyone can gain from being polite and considerate. For the college graduate, good manners will result in a faster climb up the ladder of success. For the CEO, a polite attitude toward his or her board of directors will result in a long list of rewards that otherwise might be slow in coming.

For the reader who learns new skills from this book, put them to work right away. The sooner you implement a new behavior, the better your chances are of making it a permanent part of your personal and professional lives.

· ·

Lessons are not given, they are taken.

—CESARE PAVES

Acknowledgments

No book is a solitary effort and I am deeply grateful to those who helped me with this one. To the men and women who attended the Protocol School of Washington seminars and trainings during my tenure: while you learned from me, I also learned from you. To Pamela Eyring for brilliantly acquiring the Protocol School of Washington in 2005 and powering it to greater heights.

To Robert Hickey, Deputy Director of the Protocol School of Washington, who helped me create the first training manual to launch the school's "Train the Trainer" curriculum in 1988. He's my "go-to guru" whose kind but frank words can bring my analytical dialogue to a halt. Our friendship dates back more than three decades to when he designed my first book, *Entertaining and Etiquette for Today*.

To the Etiquette and Leadership Institute trio, Debra Lassiter, Cindy Haygood, and April McLean. This dream team acquired my Youth Division curriculum in 2006 and added enormous depth to it.

This book never would have been written without the calm assistance of someone who has always been in my corner—Ann Noyes. She is my friend, my pull-it-together ally, and my beloved niece, and she has played a major role in my etiquette and protocol projects.

To my agent, John Steele, for taking me on, and guiding both Liv and me with an essence of calm and cool. You will always be our hero!

To Liv Tyler, my beloved granddaughter whom I cherish, for adding her wisdom to *Modern Manners*.

Deep gratitude to Pam Krauss, my publisher at Clarkson Potter. You placed me in the hands of an excellent team: my editor, Aliza Fogelson, and my designer, Rae Ann Spitzenberger, who both exhibited enormous patience with me and my schedule. They also connected me to the amazing Julia Rothman, whose illustrations brought these pages to life. Of course, the book could not have been completed without the supportive talent at Clarkson Potter: Amy Boorstein, Emma Brodie, Maureen Clark, Doris Cooper, Jessica Freeman-Slade, Mark McCauslin, Jane Treuhaft, and Kim Tyner.

Finally, my thanks go to everyone who has been a part of my life: my beautiful daughter, Bebe Buell, who along with Steven Tyler added an incredibly exciting element—plus, they produced Liv Tyler. And my family and my friends, who in one way or another made this book possible.

References

Brown, Robert E., and Dorothea Johnson. *The Protocol School of Washington: The Power of Handshaking—For Peak Performance Worldwide.* Sterling, Va.: Capital Book, Inc., 2004.

Hickey, Robert. *The Protocol School of Washington's Honor & Respect: The Official Guide to Names, Titles & Forms of Address.* Washington, D.C.: The Protocol School of Washington, 2008.

Johnson, Dorothea. *The Little Book of Etiquette: From the Protocol School of Washington.* Philadephia: The Running Press, 1997, 2010.

Johnson, Dorothea, and Bruce Richardson. *The Protocol School of Washington: Tea and Etiquette—Taking Tea for Business and Pleasure.* Danville, Ky.: Benjamin Press, 2009.

Recommended Books

Crane & Company. *The Blue Book of Stationery.* Boston: Crane & Co., Inc., 2009.

French, Mary Mel. *United States Protocol: The Guide to Official Diplomatic Etiquette.* New York: Rowman & Littlefield Publishers, 2010.

Goleman, Daniel. *Social Intelligence: The Revolutionary New Science of Human Relationships.* New York: Bantam Books, 2006.

Index